IRELAND
A Very
Peculiar
History

'If you're lucky
enough to be
Irish, then
you're lucky
enough.'

For Ewan and Daniel,
two Irish Pipes!

Editor: Tanya Kant
Additional artwork: Michael Tickner

Published in Great Britain in MMIX by
Book House, an imprint of
The Salariya Book Company Ltd
25 Marlborough Place, Brighton BN1 1UB
www.salariya.com
www.book-house.co.uk

HB ISBN-13: 978-1-905638-98-7

1 3 5 7 9 8 6 4 2
A CIP catalogue record for this book is available
from the British Library.
Printed and bound in Malta.
Printed on paper from sustainable sources.

IRELAND
A Very
Peculiar
History

Jim Pipe

'All the world's a stage and
most of us are desperately
unrehearsed.'
Sean O'Casey

Created and designed by
David Salariya

Illustrated by
Craig Howarth

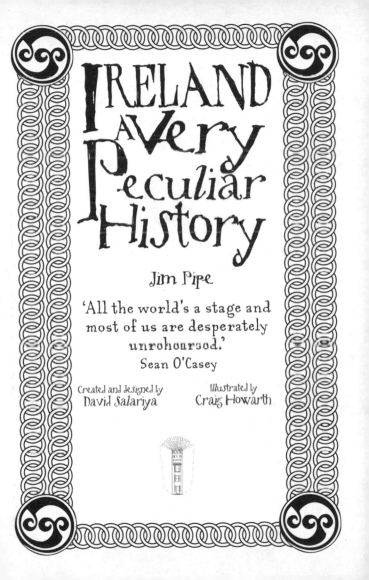

'The Irish gave the bagpipes to the Scots as a joke, but the Scots haven't seen the joke yet.'
Oliver Herford

'We have always found the Irish a bit odd. They refuse to be English.'
Winston Churchill

'Everywhere I go I'm asked if I think the university stifles writers. My opinion is that they don't stifle enough of them. There's many a best-seller that could have been prevented by a good teacher.'
Flannery O'Connor

Contents

Ten things to thank the Irish for   6

Putting Ireland on the map   8

Some very peculiar facts   10

Chapter one: Ireland emerges from the mist   11

Chapter two: Invasion!   43

Chapter three: The English take charge   71

Chapter four: Catholics vs. Protestants   96

Chapter five: A nation reborn   128

Chapter six: One island, two states   146

Recipe for Crubeens   168

Timeline of Irish history   170

Celtic names   183

Index   186

Ten things to thank the Irish for

If you thought Guinness was the only great Irish invention, think again:

1. **Submarines** – In 1881 John Holland invented a three-man submarine, which was used by Fenian rebels to try and sink British ships. The Fenians tried to steal it after they fell out with Holland, but only Holland knew how it worked.

2. **Injections** – In 1845, Francis Rynd invented the first syringe at Meath Hospital in Dublin.

3. **H_2O** – William Higgins (1763–1825) invented a system of letters to identify chemicals, such as H for Hydrogen and O for Oxygen.

4. **Bacon rashers** – In 1820, Henry Denny discovered that sandwiching long pieces of bacon between two layers of dry salt helped preserve the meat.

5. **'Bureaucracy'** – The word was first coined by the Irish writer, Lady Morgan (1776–1859).

6. **Flavoured crisps** – Invented by Joe Murphy, the first cheese and onion crisp was developed in 1954.

7. **The ejector seat** – Much loved by pilots and James Bond, the ejector seat was invented in 1946 by Irish engineer, Sir James Martin.

8. **Irish coffee** – Barman Joe Sheridan invented this mix of coffee, sugar, whiskey and thick cream as a pick-me-up for shivering transatlantic pilots at Foynes airport in the early 1940s (see page 153).

9. **Blue skies** – OK, so Irish scientist John Tyndell (1820–1893) didn't invent skies – but he did work out what makes them blue (dust in the air scatters the Sun's blue rays). Tyndell also invented the modern foghorn and his light pipe led to the development of fibre optics.

10. **Wind speed** – In 1805, Irishman Sir Francis Beaufort developed a way of describing how windy it was outside – still known as the Beaufort scale.

Putting Ireland on the map

Key:

1. Neolithic settlers appear, 7000BC
2. Scots settlers arrive, 1515
3. Launch of the *Titanic*, Belfast, 1912
4. Battle of the Yellow Ford, Co. Armagh, 1598
5. Battle of the Boyne, Drogheda, 1690
6. The Vikings arrive, 760
7. Grace O'Malley's (1530–1600) pirate ship
8. Turoe stone, Bulluan, Co. Galway
9. Battle of Clontarf, Dublin, 1014
10. The *Yankee Clipper* arrives at Foynes Airport, 1939
11. Ogham stones of Co. Kerry, c. 500
12. Cabbage Patch Revolution, Co. Tipperary, 1849
13. Norman Invasion begins, 1160s
14. Battle of Vinegar Hill, Co. Wexford, 1798
15. Copper mining, Co. Cork, 1800–1500 BC
16. French ships threaten off the coast of
    Bantry, Co. Cork, 1796

Londonderry
(Derry)
②

①

Donegal

Sligo

NORTHERN
IRELAND

Belfast
④

⑤

③

⑥

⑦

REPUBLIC OF
IRELAND

⑨

Dublin

Galway

⑧

✈ ⑩

⑫

⑪

Limerick

⑬

Waterford

⑭

Cork

⑯   ⑮

Wexford

N

Some very peculiar facts

- Ireland's famous natural landmark, the Giant's Causeway, found off the cliffs on the coast of North Antrim, is made up of around 40,000 hexagonal basalt columns. Legend has it that Finn MacCool laid the honeycomb-like columns as a pathway to reach his love on Staffa island, Scotland, where the columns are also found.

- One of Irishman Latham Valentine Blacker's military inventions, the Hedgehog, showered mortar bombs at its target. It destroyed some 50 German submarines during World War II.

- In 2007, the inhabitants of the islands of Inis Mor and Inis Oirr clashed in a bid to crown themselves 'the real Craggy Island' – Craggy Island being the fictional setting of the Irish TV sitcom, *Father Ted*. The dispute was settled in front of thousands of fans by a football match at 'The Friends of Father Ted' festival. Inis Mor took the hallowed prize after a 2–0 win.

- At a whopping twenty-two letters in length, County Galway's small village of Muckanaghederdauhaulia ('Murceanach idir Dhá Sháile' in Irish) is thought to be the longest place name in Ireland.

CHAPTER ONE

IRELAND
EMERGES FROM THE MIST

An icy start

efore you stretches mile after mile of unbroken snow and ice. Not an animal or plant is in sight, and the eerie silence of this bleak wilderness is broken only by the howling winds of an Arctic storm.

Europe is in the grip of an Ice Age and most of Ireland lies buried beneath a giant sheet of ice.[1] Deep below the surface, the shifting ice grinds against the land, carving out the smooth mountains and U-shaped valleys that will give Ireland its characteristic beauty. It will take thousands of years for the ice to

1 The weight of the ice sheet pressed the land down by several metres. Once it had melted, the north of Ireland began to rise again. Malin Head in Co. Donegal is still rising by 2 to 3mm per year!

retreat. Tough grasses will spread across the land and by 11,000 BC, the first trees will appear. Little by little, the polar desert will become the 'Emerald Isle' we recognise today.

The hush of the Ice Age was broken by the grunts, roars and squeaks of giant elk and the host of other animals that crossed the land bridge connecting Ireland with Britain and the rest of Europe. As the ice melted, sea levels rose. Around 12,000 years ago, the Irish Sea, then an enormous freshwater lake, was flooded with sea water. Four thousand years later, the waters of the North Sea swamped the land bridge with Europe, and Ireland became an island.

Ireland 12,000 years ago

Ireland

Britain

Land bridge connecting
Ireland and Britain

The first Irish rovers

Making the most of the warmer weather, Stone Age[2] hunters spread north from France into Britain. Ireland, perched on the edge of the Atlantic Ocean, was the next step. They arrived in Ireland around 7000 BC, wading through shallow waters or sailing from southern Scotland in boats made from animal skins.

As hunter-gatherers, these people were always on the move, in search of their next meal.[3] One such band stopped at Mount Sandel in County Derry. Their domed mobile homes were made from bent wooden poles covered with animal skins and leafy branches, with a warming fire at the centre. They were tidy folk, depositing their rubbish in pits at the edge of the camp.

The remains found in these rubbish pits tell us that the first Irish men and women hunted boar, duck and wood pigeon using flint weapons.

2 The hunter-gatherers were Middle Stone Age or Mesolithic people; while new farmers were New Stone Age, or Neolithic.
3 They certainly got around, popping up in Lough Boora (Co. Offaly), Woodpark (Co. Sligo) and Mount Sandel.

'If you think this is big, you should see the one that got away!'

The dogs they hunted with sometimes became 'emergency rations'. They also had a taste for hazelnuts, wild plums, salmon and eels. Living in small family and tribal groups, they shared everything. Though life was tough, these people found there was time to develop the age-old Irish love of games, banter and laughter.

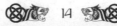

Settling down

Around 6500 BC, a new wave of settlers arrived in Ireland. Some leap-frogged along the coasts of Spain and France in boats made from animal skins, while others trekked across Europe from the Middle East. Though few in number, the newcomers transformed Ireland forever with their big idea: farming.

These 'blow-ins'[4] showed the locals how to grow exotic crops such as barley and wheat, and how to keep goats, sheep and cattle. They also brought some clever gadgets: advanced stone cutting tools, pots for storing water, and polished stone axes[5] to clear forests for farming. It took a couple of thousand years, but by 4500 BC, Ireland was a land of farmers.[6] The Céide Fields in County Mayo, built around 3700 BC, had long stone walls which divided herds of cattle into neat pens. Home to 500 people, Céide was the biggest cattle ranch in Stone Age Europe.

4 Blow-ins: an Irish expression for foreigners.
5 Some axes were made from a hard stone called porcellanite and were traded with people in Britain.
6 The hunter-gatherers weren't wiped out, they just changed their ways: DNA tests reveal that over 75 per cent of Irish people today are related to these first inhabitants.

Loot on legs

In ancient Ireland, there was a lot more to cattle than meat, milk and leather. Owning a fine herd of cows was a sign of great wealth and made you a 'bóaire', or 'lord of cows'. In the famous Táin saga, when Medb, the powerful queen of Connacht, wants to prove to her husband Ailill how fabulously rich she is, she steals the brown bull of Cooley, Ulster's finest beast. Cattle rustling remained something of an Irish national sport[7] well into the 20th century.

Queen Mebd was always keen on russelling up a fresh meal.

[7] Cattle rustling was often made easier by farmers herding their cows away from the ranch to higher pastures in the summer, a practice known as 'booleying'.

Riddle of the tombs

The Stone Age Irish put a great deal of effort and skill into building enormous stone tombs. Over 1,000 megalithic[8] tombs survive, scattered all over Ireland. The giant stones we see today were once covered with mounds of grass, earth and rubble, so from the air the tombs would have looked like green, hairy flying saucers.

It remains a mystery how the huge stones (weighing some 100 tons) were hauled into place or what they were used for. If they were a key to the Stone Age 'Otherworld', why were bodies often cremated or buried above ground? Perhaps the tombs were used for tribal rituals. The tomb at Newgrange, County Meath, built in 3200 BC (500 years before the Great Pyramid), is one of the world's oldest time-pieces. On the 21st of December (the first day of the solar year, celebrated by many ancient cultures as the Winter Solstice) the morning sun is at just the right angle to shine down the dark passageway. It lights up the burial chamber 20 metres inside for just 9 minutes.

8 *Megalithic means 'great stone' in Greek.*

The tomb-spotter's guide

How to spot a megalithic tomb:

Court tombs have giant stones placed in a semicircle at the entrance, leading to burial chambers within.

Portal tombs have two tall stones at the front, a lower stone at the back, and a massive stone slab on top. The enormous portal tomb at Poulnabrone in County Clare had more than 20 people buried in it over a 60-year period.

Wedge-shaped tombs are high at the front and short and squat at the back. Hag's Bed in County Cork gets its name from the skeleton of a headless woman found in it when it was first opened.

Passage tombs, such as at Newgrange, have a long passage leading to an inner chamber. Many have mysterious swirling patterns carved around the entrance.

Passage tomb

The Bronze Age

Around 2500 BC, another band of settlers, the 'Beaker folk',[9] arrived on Irish shores, dazzling the locals with their knowledge of metalworking. Copper was mined from Mount Gabriel in County Cork from 1800 to 1500 BC. Later, Irish ships made the journey to Cornwall, England, for tin which they mixed with copper to make into bronze. Pots and pans were improved, and weapons became a lot tougher – they needed to be!

A lot of fighting was going on in Ireland at this time, interrupted only by unusually soggy weather, plagues and famines. Around 1000 BC, Irish warriors began to fight on chariots or from horseback, though without saddles or stirrups it must have been hard to swing a sword without falling off. Dún Aonghasa on the island of Inish Mór was one of many hillforts first built in this era. Its thick walls give an idea of just how nervous everyone felt about the threat of attack.

---

9 The Beaker folk got their name from the distinctive beakers (cups) often found in their graves.

Fashion was changing too. Metal was the 'new stone', and powerful chieftains, wealthy from the farming revolution, festooned themselves with fancy collars, earrings, necklaces and even capes made from gold. Ireland may even have had its own gold rush thanks to mines in the hills of County Wicklow. For a short while, jewellery was even made from solid gold bars rather than thin sheets.

When in doubt, wear gold!

The mysterious Celts

The next big shake-up came with the arrival of the Celts. These warlike people from Spain were armed with iron weapons. Small bands of Celts came to Ireland in dribs and drabs, starting around 600 BC. They made a big impression, and not just because they rushed into battle naked, save for the torques (metal collars) around their necks. Celtic ways were quickly adopted by the locals and after a few generations it became hard to tell who was who.

The Celts remain something of a mystery, however, because they never wrote anything down. We know a bit about them from their enemies, the Romans, who dismissed them as a wild, drunken bunch who ate their own fathers. The Celts did enjoy a party – wines were shipped in from the Mediterranean – and they were undoubtedly fierce and fearless. Urged on by pipers and a howling mob, Celtic warriors rode into battle on chariots, clanging their weapons against the sides. They also hung noisy rattles (shaped like hand grenades) from their horses to terrify their opponents.

However, for a supposedly wild bunch, the Celts were remarkably well organised. They built highways for their carts and chariots, called *sligthi* – the first step towards Irish motorways. Celtic tribes also divided Ireland into five provinces. Four of these remain today:

- Munster – the south-west
- Ulster – the north
- Connacht – the west
- Leinster – the south-east, which merged with the fifth province, Meath (the centre)

Ireland

Ulster

Connacht

Meath

Part of Leinster

Leinster

Munster

Headhunters

The Celts believed a person's soul was in his or her head, so after battle, Celtic warriors lopped off their enemies' heads, slung them from their chariots and brought them to the victory feast.

There was no legal system as such, but people followed a set of rules known as Brehon Law, which dealt with everything from murder to the way apples fell in autumn. According to one law, a chief had to be 'complete', so rivals tried to gouge out each other's eyes! In legend, when the leader of the Tuatha Dé Danaan, Nuada, lost an arm in battle, he could no longer be king. The quick-thinking Nuada replaced it with a shiny arm made of silver and was crowned king once more.

Swirls and stories

The Irish Celts, or *Gaels*[10] as they became known, produced some stunning art. They carved and painted beautiful swirling loops onto leather, sword handles and standing stones, though no-one today knows for sure what these patterns mean. Celtic burial sites are also full of decorated pins used to fasten tunics and cloaks. The Celts also spoke the language that became Irish.[11] Celtic languages were spoken across much of Europe, and the Celts were well connected: blue beads from Egypt and amber from Scandanavia have turned up in Celtic graves on the hill of Tara, while the skeleton of a Barbary ape from Spain was found on the site of the Navan ringfort, dating from 200 BC.

The beautifully carved Turoe stone in Ballaun, Co. Galway

10 The word Gael *may in fact be Welsh, meaning 'wild' or 'savage'.*
11 The Celtic word for Ireland, Ierne *or* Eriu, *became the modern* Éire.

No Celtic feast was complete without a good story. Any chieftain worth his salt filled his court with bards, poets and storytellers, who learned hundreds of tales by heart. Their songs and stories ensured that the chieftain's heroic deeds would live on. If the chieftain didn't pay for his story, he risked becoming the villain of the tale. The epic tales of the hero Cúchulainn from the Táin saga give us an idea of life at court in the first few centuries AD – a life of feasts, cattle raids and love affairs.

How to spot a Celt

Looks : fair hair and blue eyes.

Hairstyle : the Celts dyed their hair with lime-wash, making it very stiff.

Tattoos : Celtic warriors used berry juice to paint their bodies blue.

Glamour : Celtic men and women loved to wear jewellery made from amber, bronze and gold. The word *glamour* originally meant the ability to change shape (into an animal), a popular trick in Celtic legends.

four heroes...

Cúchulainn is a hero from the Tain Saga. His name means 'Hound of Culann', as he killed the blacksmith Culann's guard-dog in self-defence, then offered to takes its place. In battle he went into a 'warp spasm' – his body turned itself inside out and fire and blood shot out of his head!

Finn MacCool, who appears in an ancient text called the Fenian cycle, was High King of Ireland during the 3rd century AD. When Finn tried to cook the Salmon of Knowledge, he burnt his fingers on the fish. Sucking his sore thumb, he swallowed some of the salmon and became a know-it-all.

Tuathal, from the 9th-century poem 'Mael Mura of Othain', was the first king of all Ireland. He was tricked into agreeing that the King of Leinster could marry both of his daughters. Tuathal didn't see the funny side – he forced the King of Leinster to hand over 15,000 cows, pigs, cauldrons and slave women in compensation.

Niall of the Nine Hostages was a real 4th-century king. He got his name from grabbing hostages from the five Irish provinces, to ensure that everyone he dealt with behaved themselves. During a raid on Britain, he kidnapped the boy who later became St Patrick, the patron saint of Ireland.

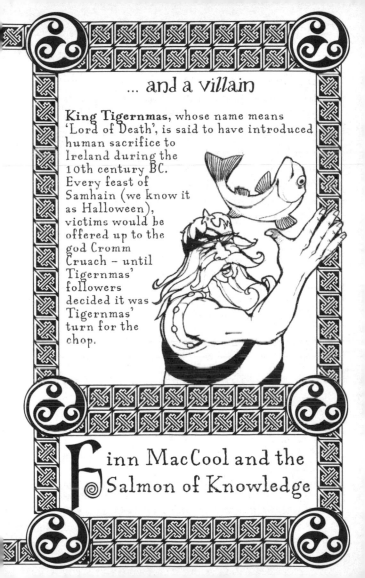

... and a villain

King Tigernmas, whose name means 'Lord of Death', is said to have introduced human sacrifice to Ireland during the 10th century BC. Every feast of Samhain (we know it as Halloween), victims would be offered up to the god Cromm Cruach – until Tigernmas' followers decided it was Tigernmas' turn for the chop.

Finn MacCool and the Salmon of Knowledge

The Celts created a culture that came to be regarded as uniquely Irish. For centuries, storytellers known as *shanachies* wandered from town to town, entertaining the locals with tales of heroes, fairies and magic. However, the Irish love of a good yarn can make it hard to tell fact from fiction. *The Book of Invasions*, penned by Irish monks in the 11th century, is a jumble of myth and history:

The first invasion of Ireland is led by none other than Noah's granddaughter Cesair, who for reasons unknown has been refused entry on board the Ark. Cesair arrives in County Cork with 50 other women and three men. When two of the men die, Fintan is the last man standing. Terrified at the thought of fathering the future population of Ireland by himself, he turns himself into a salmon and swims for dear life. Sadly, Cesair dies from a broken heart and the rest of the party, now without men, go the way of the dinosaurs.

The next invaders wisely wait until after the Flood, only to be wiped out by a plague. They're followed by the Fomorians, giants who live on Tory Island off the north coast, and the Fir Bolg, or bag men, who carry around magic earth in leather bags. Neither of these are a match, however, for the all-powerful Tuatha Dé Danaan, 'children of the Goddess Danu', who are skilled in magic. The Tuatha are eventually defeated by yet more invaders, the Milesians. They are driven underground and live as fairy people in the megalithic tombs dotted around Ireland.

These stories about mythical tribes are probably inspired by different groups of Celts arriving in Ireland, but it's hard to be sure what's fact and what's fiction.

While the Irish Celts were busy raiding and partying, the Romans were conquering the rest of Europe (and a lot more besides). They made it as far as the east coast of Wales but decided that was far enough. Perhaps someone warned them about the weather in Ireland: the Romans called Ireland *Hibernia*, the 'Land of Winter'.

Celtic Ireland was divided into about 150 kingdoms, called *tuatha*, each ruled by a local king or chieftain. These chieftains spent a lot of time stealing cattle from each other, but some learned that co-operating with your neighbours made life easier for everyone. A few even earned enough support to call themselves High Kings of Ireland, though they never had control over a very large area.

By now, most Irish people were speaking a form of Celtic. The first Irish words can be traced back to Ogham, a simple form of writing that was carved onto stone. Each letter was made up from marks of slashes, a sort of gaelic morse code. Ogham inscriptions appear on standing stones found near ancient religious sites. Some are solitary while others appear in mysterious circles, ovals or horseshoe formation. About 400 Ogham stones remain, many in Munster.

This one says 'Mór', which means 'Great'.

The shrieking stone

Tara, a hill in County Meath, was the ceremonial capital of Irish kings during the first millennium, though some of the surrounding burial mounds may date back to 4000 BC. No kings lived at Tara, but they gathered their armies around the hill before marching to war. Tara was also the home of the Stone of Destiny, which in legend shrieked when the feet of the true king rested on it.

You can get off whenever you like, you know.

Shriek... what real royal feat!

The endless cattle raids meant that the Celts took to living near ringforts (protected, circular-shaped settlements), hillforts or in *crannogs* – fortified houses built on man-made islands. The ringfort at Emain Macha in County Armagh was home to the kings of Ulster, while Medb, the queen of Connacht, had her own fort in Rathcroghan, County Roscommon. In Brehon law, women had the same rights as men, including going to war: the mythical hero Cúchulainn was trained to fight by three women.

Cúchulainn – fighting fit

Saints and snakes

To the Celts, the gods were everywhere – in the sky, on mountain tops, in trees, lakes and rivers.[12] The Celts' bearded, white-robed priests, the Druids, had real power: even kings listened to them. They claimed they could see into the future by watching flocks of birds, and they dabbled in magic, so few dared to disagree with their predictions.

Things changed again with the arrival of St Patrick in the late 5th century. At this time, Irish chieftains carried out regular raids on Roman Britain, taking booty and slaves.[13] Patrick was kidnapped in one of these raids at the age of 16, and later found God while minding sheep as a slave in the hills of County Antrim. Though there were already a few Christians in Ireland, St Patrick had a tough conversion job ahead of him. Luckily, Patrick was a great storyteller, using a three-leaved

12 *The Celts were eager to please their gods: a single bog in Offaly revealed 177 swords, spears and axes, thrown into the water as tributes over many years.*
13 *The Irish were very successful pirates. In AD 401 a fleet of black Irish currachs (small ships) swept up the coast of Britain and seized 'many thousands' of prisoners.*

shamrock[14] to explain the mystery of the Holy Trinity. He wowed the locals with displays of relics and miracles, and also convinced people that they probably wouldn't be struck down by a plague of warts for ignoring the Druids.

A real charmer?

St Patrick is said to have driven the snakes out of Ireland. It's a good story but complete nonsense! Snakes were one of many animals (including moles, polecats and weasels) that didn't make it to Ireland when the land bridge with England existed. Perhaps these legendary snakes symbolise the Celtic god Dagda being chased out of the country. The myth may be based on the Viking word *Padrekr*, which means 'toad-chucker out', and is pretty close to the Irish form of Patrick – Padraig.

---

14 *What we call a 'shamrock' is actually four different species of plant that look alike.*

Celtic gods and goddesses

Dagda: King of the gods. Dagda carried a club that could kill people – or bring them back to life.

Lug: The Sun god and Cúchulainn's father.

Dian Cecht: The healing god. If someone was badly wounded, their friends threw them into a well. Dian Cecht then healed their injuries by singing down to them.

Donn: God of the dead. Druids claimed they were related to him.

Brigid: Confusingly there were three sister goddesses all called Brigid, linked with fertility, crafts and healing, respectively.

Babd: Babd could look like a beautiful woman, an old hag or a crow. Babd often appeared with her sisters Mórrígan and Macha, and this terrible trio loved to stir up trouble.

Dagda

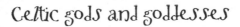

St Patrick was a cunning politician: he based himself close to Emain Macha, home of the Ulster kings, while his bishops were based near Tara and Medb's ancient capital in Connacht. This tactic worked: the kings that St Patrick converted stayed loyal to Christianity and over the next 200 years, most Irish people became Christian.

Ireland didn't forget its pagan past, however. The Irish continue to celebrate pagan festivals such as May Day and Halloween, and up until the 12th century a husband and wife could call it quits and separate for good on 1st February, the feast of the pagan god Imbolc.

Medieval divorce

Spreading the word

6th-century monastery

From the mid-6th century AD onwards monasteries sprang up all over Ireland. The Irish, who were beginning to develop reading and writing systems, set about copying anything and everything they could get their hands on. The monasteries trained monks to become brilliant scribes, artists and thinkers. They created masterpieces such as the Book of Kells and the stunning metalwork of the silver Ardagh Chalice.

Colum Cille (St Columbus)
gives Nessy a fright.

Irish monks spread the Christian message far and wide. Colum Cille (also know as St. Columba) set off with a dozen disciples to found a new monastery on the Scottish island of Iona; his followers later set up monasteries all over Britain and Europe. In AD 565, according to one legend, he also saved a swimmer from the Loch Ness monster, scaring it away with his booming voice.

The first books

Irish monks came up with a new kind of book, the codex, which replaced the scroll. The codex was made from dried sheepskin, folded in half, making it taller than it was wide and so giving us the shape of a modern book. The monks also fused Latin and Greek alphabets with Ogham script and the spirals and zigzags found on ancient tombs.

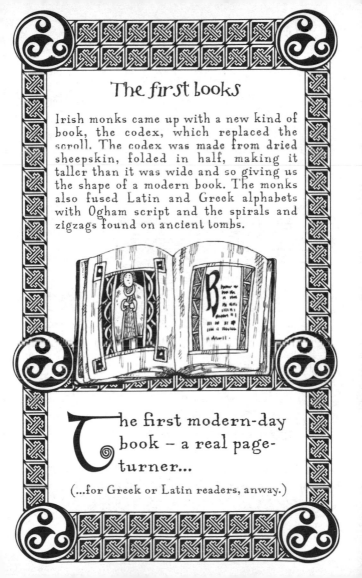

The first modern-day book – a real page-turner...

(...for Greek or Latin readers, anway.)

IRELAND A VERY PECULIAR HISTORY

Back in Ireland, another group of monks founded a monastery on Skellig Michael, a bare pyramid of rock lying off the coast of Kerry. They lived in beehive-shaped huts high above the stormy Atlantic waters, dining on seabirds and fertilising their gardens with seaweed.

Skillig Michael's monks had a fine flock of soon-to-be books.

In Kildare, the abbess Brigid founded a monastery under a giant oak tree.[15] Brigid became one of Ireland's best-loved saints. Saints were so popular that their body parts were kept as relics – St Kieran asked for his body to be left on a hilltop so that it would be eaten by animals before the locals could get their hands on it.

He'd make a nice relic...

St Kieran

But these holy men and women had quite a job on their hands if they wanted to change traditional ways. Slavery was still common, despite St Patrick's best efforts to stop it: six cows bought you a female slave. If a chieftain wanted his neighbours' land, he would simply march in and take it. Sadly, the new faith didn't stop the Irish fighting among themselves.

15 *Giving the county its name:* Kildare *means 'church of the oak'.*

All for a good cause

In such violent times, it's amazing that no Irish martyrs died for their faith. To make up for this, holy Irish men and women found other ways to show their dedication:

- **White martyrs** showed their faith by leaving Ireland to spread the word (not so bad, given the weather). St Brendan is said to have reached America in a tiny boat called a currach. He also found the time to curse 50 Irish rivers.

- **Green martyrs** were people who left home to live out in the wild. St Kevin lived up a tree for a while (where a blackbird laid on egg on his hand), then upgraded to a cave. He spent his days standing naked in a freezing lake or flinging himself into a patch of stinging nettles.

- **St Brigid** was said to have blinded herself in one eye to put off potential husbands, so she could devote herself to God. In another legend she changed her bath water into beer. No wonder she was so popular!

- **St Comgall** founded the great monastery at Bangor after living as a hermit on the shore of Lough Erne. In legend, he could shatter rocks with his magic spit!

CHAPTER TWO

INVASION!

Norse raiders

hough Irish monks did their best to light up the Dark Ages with their illuminated texts, things were about to get much darker. In 795 AD, Viking raiders looted Colum Cille's monastery on the island of Iona then, sailing further south, attacked Rathlin island off the coast of County Antrim. Over the next 200 years, these well-armed, bloodthirsty raiders from Norway and Denmark scared the living daylights out of the Irish.

To begin with, small fleets of Viking longboats carried out sneaky attacks on Irish monasteries, which were full to the brim with treasures. Monasteries doubled up as trading centres, so

craftsmen and farmers were plundered into the bargain. The monks were no strangers to raids by Irish chieftains, but these new attackers were ferocious, bloody and unexpected. When Vikings ransacked and burnt Bangor monastery in 888, they slaughtered some 700 people, including the abbot and monks.

Lock up your treasures, the Vikings are coming.

The round towers

Built around AD950, this tall stone tower belonged not to Rapunzel but to the monks of Glendalough monastery in Co. Wicklow. It was a store for holy treasure, a lookout and a refuge from raiders all rolled into one – the door is 3 metres from the ground and the monks climbed in and out using a long ladder. Round towers like this can be seen all over Ireland.

Maximum security monastery.

While the Irish kings were busy fighting each other, the Vikings grew bolder. By the 9th century, large Viking fleets were travelling inland. The Vikings started to put down roots: in the winter of AD 840. These *Ostmen* ('men from the East'), as they called themselves, set up a permanent ship's camp[1] on the banks of the River Liffey, which became the Viking headquarters. Its name, Dublin, comes from the Irish words Dubh Linn, meaning 'black pool'.

The first Irish towns

The Vikings were keen sailors and preferred trading to farming. For the next 150 years, they mostly kept to themselves or sailed off in search of fresh adventures in Britain and Iceland. Indeed, as their settlements in Dublin, Wexford, Waterford, Cork and Limerick grew into Ireland's first towns, the Vikings proved to be very useful neighbours. They brought the latest ship-building skills, talented artists and craftsmen, and also coinage. Irish words for boat, market and beer all originate from Norse.

---

1 A Viking ship's camp was a 'long phort' – which gives us the name for the Irish county of Longford.

The little people

Small and somewhat wrinkly male fairies, called leprechauns, were said to guard the treasure left behind by marauding Vikings, which they buried in crocks (pottery containers) or pots. They and other fairy folk were thought to be the spirits of the ancient Tuatha Dé Danaan people that live in ancient ruins and tombs. In Irish legend, if you catch a leprechaun he will hand over his pot of gold when you promise to let him go – but watch him closely or he'll vanish in the blink of an eye. Believers should also keep an eye out for:

• **Banshees** – female ancestors that wail terribly when someone in the family dies.

• **Pooka** – a terrifying spirit that appears as an eagle, goat or horse and has a nasty habit of taking lost travellers on midnight rides.

• **Selkies** – gentle spirits that are humans by day and seals at night.

• **Changelings** – fairy children swapped for stolen human babies. To stop this from happening, mothers would smash a potato against the hearth.

All in all, the Vikings were a lot friendlier after they had settled down – they even pitched in when rival Irish chieftains went to war. However, the Vikings still weren't particularly welcome and in AD 902 the Ostmen were pushed out of Dublin. Warlike as ever, they returned with a huge fleet in AD 914 and quickly recaptured the port. This time the Vikings had big plans for Dublin: they built a new town 3 kilometres closer to the sea, laying out streets and houses and even putting in drains.

By the late 10th century, Dublin was buzzing. It was home to 10,000 people and its streets were thronged with craftsmen selling goods fashioned from wood, bone and leather. Foreign traders flocked to Dublin to buy and sell in one of the biggest slave markets in western Europe. The Vikings also sold furs and hides to England and imported luxury goods from all over the known world: silk from the East, silver from Germany and amber from the Baltic Sea.

Having all these foreigners on their doorstep encouraged the Irish to unite (at last) and they defeated the Vikings at the Battle of Tara in AD 980. Twenty-five years later, the king of Munster, BrianBorú,[2] had won enough battles against rival chieftains to call himself High King of Ireland. When the Ostmen of Dublin joined in a rebellion againstBorú, he marched north and crushed them at the Battle of Clontarf[3] in AD 1014.

The Vikings were no longer a threat to the Irish. Large numbers stayed in Ireland, but from now on they kept a low profile: many took Irish wives and became Christians. In Dublin, they were forced to make a new home for themselves north of the River Liffey. Dubliners today joke that 'Northsiders' are a rowdy bunch – perhaps it's their Viking roots!

Sadly for Ireland, BrianBorú was killed by a fleeing Viking at Clontarf. The Irish chieftains went back to squabbling among themselves, though they found time to punish Brian's killer, tying him to a tree using his own intestines.

2 BrianBorú was from the Kennedy clan, so he is a distant relative of US President, John F. Kennedy!
3 Today, Clontarf is a suburb in north Dublin.

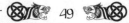

Seven of the worst

In the dog-eat-dog world of the Dark Ages, a powerful curse was worth its weight in gold. In one legend, the kings of Tara had a cursing match with Saint Ruadhan. Ruadhan won and turned Tara into a barren wilderness. Here are some favourite Irish curses:

May six horse-loads of graveyard clay
fall on top of you.

May snails devour your dead body and the rains
rot it away.

May the Devil swallow you sideways.

May you go blind so that you can't tell your wife
from a haystack.

May you be afflicted with the itch and have no
nails to scratch with.

May you melt off the earth like
snow off the ditch.

The Norman conquest

By AD 1100, no king was strong enough to take the title of High King of Ireland. As the 12th century unfolded, two of the most powerful chieftains in Ireland, Dermot MacMurrough (King of Leinster) and Tiernan O'Rourke (King of Breffni) battled for the title for 14 years. MacMurrough made matters worse when he kidnapped O'Rourke's wife in AD 1152, (though it has been suggested she was happy to go with him). When O'Rourke got support from Rory O'Connor, the King of Connacht, MacMurrough was forced to flee from Ireland.

MacMurrough sailed to France to seek help from the Norman king of England, Henry II – and changed the course of Irish history. The Normans were tough, well-organised and ruthless. Originally Viking raiders, they had settled in north-west France in the 9th century. By 1100 they also ruled England and southern Italy and were setting up crusader states in Palestine. Henry II had already thought about invading Ireland in the 1150s and was happy to lend MacMurrough enough money to pay for an army of Norman soldiers. MacMurrough found recruits in South Wales, led by Richard FitzGilbert de Clare, nicknamed 'Strongbow' as his army relied on Welsh archers.

Strongbow's army

MacMurrough returned to Ireland with a small force in August 1167 and offered Tiernan O'Rourke 100 ounces of gold in compensation for having stolen his wife. Strongbow finally arrived in May 1169 to support MacMurrough. With 1,000 men and 200 knights Strongbow wasted no time in capturing Irish lands in the south-east. The Irish warriors, some armed only with stones and slings, were no match for the Norman

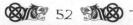

knights, who fought from horseback and were equipped with steel weapons and armour. When Strongbow's captain, Hervey de Monte Marisco, captured Waterford in August 1170, he cut off the heads, arms and legs of its 70 leaders and flung their bodies over a cliff. Strongbow paused to marry MacMurrough's daughter Aoife, then marched north. The Vikings of Dublin surrendered when Strongbow and his men surged into the city, and the Viking leaders wisely jumped in their longships and fled to the Isle of Man.

The Emerald Isle

During the 12th century, Irish bishops tried to free themselves from the rule of the English Church. When the English clergy complained to Pope Adrian IV (also an Englishman), he gave Henry II permission to invade Ireland. The Pope is said to have sent Henry an emerald ring as a token of this agreement. Some believe this is why Ireland is called the 'Emerald Isle' (though it may have more to do with its lush, green landscape).

The castle builders

When MacMurrough died in May 1171, Strongbow became the new ruler of Leinster. Worried that Strongbow was getting too big for his boots, Henry II stepped in and claimed Ireland for himself, though he allowed Strongbow to keep Leinster as a reward. However, Strongbow did not enjoy his prize for long – he died in 1176, due to 'mortification of the foot', said to be the result of a curse by St Brigid, whose churches he had looted.

Most Irish chieftains accepted Henry II as king, hoping to avoid having their lands taken by his Norman leaders. How wrong they were – soon all of Meath was taken by force and handed over to Henry's best friend, Hugh de Lacy. When Henry returned to England, things went from bad to worse. Many of the Norman nobles had borrowed big amounts of money to pay their soldiers. They needed land to pay off their debts – and fast. They found the quickest way to make money was to murder several Irish kings, including Tiernan O'Rourke, who was tricked into an ambush

in 1172. O'Rourke's head and headless corpse were put on display on the walls of Dublin Castle, as an example to other would-be rebels.

The Norman nobles went about their business with ruthless efficiency, building a string of castles as they pushed west.[4] They launched raids on local Irish kings from these fortresses. Worn down by the attacks, many kings surrendered and their lands were handed over to Norman knights. Soon very little of the fertile farming land in the east was left in Irish hands.

New towns such as Drogheda, Sligo, Kilkenny and Trim sprang up, their high city walls another sign of Norman might. In the countryside, forests were cleared for the new Norman system of farming. Irish peasants, now without land to rear their cattle, were at the mercy of their Norman landlords, who bled them dry with taxes. The Normans knew how to make money: in 13th-century Ireland, business boomed.

4 By 1500 there were over 3,000 castles in Ireland, some of them owned by Irish chieftains. They were easy to defend but draughty and uncomfortable.

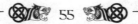

10 things animal lovers would rather not know about Ireland!

While the Irish are traditionally a nation of animal lovers, over the years some creatures have had a rough time of things in Ireland:

- **Rabbits** –These were introduced to Ireland by the Normans, not as pets but for meat and fur. They were farmed in large warrens and by 1600, Ireland exported 2 million rabbit skins each year.

- **Wolves** – To get rid of wolves that were killing their livestock, Irish farmers in the Middle Ages placed fishhooks inside a rotting body. The wolf would tear itself to pieces as it gulped the flesh down.

- **Horses** – Irish farmers tied their ploughs to horses' tails until it was banned by law in 1635.

- **Sheep** – The same law also banned farmers from pulling the wool off live sheep.

- **Cats** – According to one story, Oliver Cromwell's soldiers gathered all the cats in Kilkenny and tied them in pairs by their tails. Then they hung the understandably irate cats over a rope. The cats fought to the death, and the final cat was beheaded.

- **Irish wolfhounds** – These were first bred by the Celts as war dogs in the first century BC. Later they were used in dogfights or to hunt wolves.

- **Basking sharks** – In the 18th and 19th centuries, basking sharks were hunted for their oil, which was used to light the streets of Dublin. The oil came from the sharks' livers, which were cut out at sea. The bodies were then dumped overboard.

- **Cattle** – In 18th-century Connacht, a secret society known as the 'Houghers' took revenge on dairy farmers (who had taken their land) by wounding the famers' cattle.

- **Bears** – Richard Martin (1754–1834), known as Humanity Dick, campaigned against the cruel sports of bear-baiting and dog-fighting. He was so angry at farmers for treating their animals badly that he fought over 100 duels with them, arguing that 'an ox cannot hold a pistol'.

- **Geese** – In 19th-century Ireland, geese were pulled up chimneys by a rope. Their flapping wings dislodged the soot.

All in a name

Irish names have their roots in all sorts of places:

- **Viking** – The Irish used the prefix 'Mac', which means 'son of'. It is often combined with Viking names. For example, the viking name Magnus became MacManus.

- **Norman** – The Irish-sounding 'Fitz' comes from the French word *fils*, meaning 'son of', while the Irish surname Power comes from the French word *pauvre*, meaning 'poor one'.

- **English** – Names such as Bruton, Bermingham and Stafford became common in Ireland during the 13th century, when English labourers were tempted to settle in Ireland because land was scarce in England. Many Dubliners at this time were from Bristol.

- **Welsh** – Names such as Wogan and Walsh come from the names of the Welsh archers who fought for Strongbow.

After they invaded Connacht in the 1230s, the Normans created English settlements as far west as County Mayo. The invaders seemed unstoppable – or were they? During the 1240s, several powerful Norman lords died without leaving sons as heirs, and their lands were divided up. The Normans began fighting among themselves and the Irish were quick to take advantage. In 1209, the O'Toole clan massacred 300 Dubliners when they went outside the city walls for their May Day party. By 1270, the suburbs of Dublin were regularly attacked by bands of Irish warriors swooping down from the Wicklow Mountains.

Norman defences

Trim castle, county Meath

The Gaels fight back

Despite their French language and customs, the Norman invaders of Ireland saw themselves as English. Just to prove it, they spent several hundred years fighting their French relatives. The Irish called the Normans 'Sassanachs' (Saxons) because England was the home of most Saxons.

Under Norman rule, life for most Irish people – the *Gaels* – was grim. They lived in flimsy houses made from clay or wattle, living on a diet of oats made into cakes.[5] Most had few rights and little education. There wasn't much to read anyway, as the educated people who might have become monks and scribes in the past now tended to be lawyers or doctors.

The Normans were not all-powerful, however. In the south and west of Ireland, life carried on much as before. Gaelic kings continued to steal each other's cattle, and many became rich by terrifying townspeople (often English settlers) into paying for the privilege of not being attacked, a fee known as 'black rent'. And there

5 *At this time, bread was a luxury food eaten only by the rich.*

was always money to be made from selling weapons stolen from the Normans.

By the mid-13th century, the Irish were confident that they could take on the Normans. In 1258, the kings of Thomond, Connacht and Ulster declared Brian O'Neill (of Tyrone) High King of Ireland. But all did not go to plan. Two years later, poor Brian was captured and killed by the Normans and his severed head was sent to London – but the tide was slowly turning.

In Ulster, Gaelic chieftains won back lands from the Normans using rugged Scots fighters known as *gallowglasses*. In 1259, 10,000 of these do-or-die warriors were part of a wedding gift given by a Scottish chief to Turlough O'Neill. Their weapon of choice was a heavy two-handed axe, up to 1.8 metres long, which could chop an enemy's head off with a single blow. Irish warriors also learned how to fight like the Normans and by the 14th century they too had steel armour.

Irish spirits finally were lifted by the Scots' defeat of the English at the Battle of

Bannockburn in 1314. A group of Irish chieftains persuaded the Scots king, Robert the Bruce, to give them a helping hand. The following year, Ulster was invaded by Robert's brother, Edward the Bruce, who joined forces with the O'Neill clan in a bid to drive out the English settlers. Edward's army was so destructive that some towns didn't recover for decades. Meanwhile the Gaelic chieftains of Connacht attacked from the west. The Normans fought back: at the Battle of Athenry in 1316 they killed five Irish kings and two years later, Edward the Bruce was slain in a fierce battle near Dundalk.

Despite this, the English grip on Ireland weakened, due to a terrible famine in 1315–17 and the Black Death in 1348–9. This gruesome plague was carried aboard ships by black rats, then passed on to humans by their fleas. Once infected, the victim's body broke out in festering black boils and then spewed out torrents of slimy 'red blood'. Most died within a few days. The plague spread rapidly in towns and ports, where most of the English settlers lived.

Tying the knot

Some ancient Irish traditions lasted through the Middle Ages. The phrase 'tying the knot' came from an ancient Celtic marriage custom, where the bride and groom had their wrists tied together.

Up until 1603, you could be married to several people at once: one woman was nicknamed 'the meeting of the three enemies' as she was married to three rival lords.

Marriage could be a costly business: in the 16th century, the Lord of Waterford handed over 80 cows, 29 horses, a pair of chessboards, a harp and various pots and pans to his bride's family.

The Irish for honeymoon is 'mi na meala', or 'the month of honey'. In old Irish custom, newlyweds would spend their first month together drinking honey wine, since honey wine was thought to improve a man's virility.

In Dublin, the Black Death wiped out half of the city. During the night, cartloads of corpses were ferried to graves outside the walls in an area still known as 'Black Pitts'. The plague also led to a famine – it was said that some Dubliners were so hungry they fed on the corpses of dead criminals hanging in the streets.

The spread of the plague was speeded up by the unhealthy state of Dublin's streets. The authorities did what they could: there were public dung-heaps and at least one public toilet. Many houses had their own cesspit to hold sewage, but human waste probably made its way onto the streets, where dogs and pigs roamed freely, spreading it further (though the pigs also helped to clean up by gobbling anything remotely edible).

Medieval Dubliners came up with a cunning plan to make the most of their rubbish: they built new quays (reinforced bits of riverbank) by dumping waste behind a series of wooden fences and stone walls. These quays made the river narrower and deeper, allowing larger ships to dock.

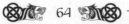

The Ice Age returns

Fourteenth century Ireland knew all about climate change – it was caught in the grip of the Little Ice Age (a cold spell that made the River Thames in London freeze over). According to one medieval document, the Annals of Connacht, one disaster followed another:

1317 A great famine kills 1 in 4 people. Reports suggest that things got so desperate that people starting eating each other!

1318 Snowfalls bury whole herds of sheep.

1322–5 The worst cattle plague on record.

1328 'Much thunder and lightning' destroys the harvest.

1335 More heavy snowfalls kill most of the small birds in Ireland.

1338 Sheep wiped out by a plague.

Too Irish by half

Natural disasters were one thing, but a bigger threat to English power was Irish women. The Irish had a long history of marrying their daughters to invaders and the Normans were happy to blend in with the locals. As a result, the invaders' children learned Irish ways from their mothers: they spoke Irish, dressed like the Gaels and played Gaelic games.

In 1366, the King of England, Edward III, was so worried about his nobles 'going native' that he sent over his son, the Duke of Clarence, to knock them into shape. Clarence passed the Kilkenny Statutes in 1366, a set of laws effectively banning Normans from mixing with the Irish. Not surprisingly, the Kilkenny Statutes were a complete failure – the nobles still married Irish women and embraced Gaelic culture. Most nobles quietly did their own thing and by the end of the 15th century the power of the English king was restricted to a small area around Dublin known as 'the Pale'. In 1495, just 330 English troops remained in Ireland.

The Kilkenny Statutes
Banned!

No speaking in Irish

No Irish dress or hairstyles
(including no moustaches or beards)

No riding like the Irish
(without saddles)

No Irish names

No marrying Irish men or women

No Irish music or storytellers

No hurling (see page 132) – The English
believed the Irish should practise their
archery (to make good soldiers), rather
than wasting their time on ball games.

The Pale was the last area of land still loyal to the English king. Outside the Pale, the English king relied on powerful Norman families to keep order – the Butlers of Ormond and the Fitzgeralds of Desmond and Kildare. Now more Irish than English, these families hated anyone from England telling them what to do – including the king. The Butlers and the Fitzgeralds were also sworn enemies of one another.

Garrett More Fitzgerald, the Earl of Kildare, governed Ireland during the reigns of five different English kings. But in 1487, soon after the new English king Henry VII had come to the throne, Fitzgerald decided to try and make a king of Lambert Simnel, a 10-year-old boy – and a complete imposter. Simnel was probably the son of a baker, but was taught by enemies of Henry VII to act like royalty, so that they could pass him off as king. The plan worked; Simnel was taken to Christ Church cathedral, Dublin, and crowned King Edward VI. Fitzgerald also backed Simnel with an army which invaded England, only to be defeated by King Henry's forces. Surprisingly, Fitzgerald was let off with little more than a slapped wrist.

A few years later, the Earl of Kildare was sacked from his job. All hell broke loose. The Butler family attacked the Fitzgeralds and gangs fought on the streets of Dublin. When the Gaelic chieftains joined in, Henry VII decided that enough was enough. He sent his deputy, Sir Edward Poynings, to clear up the mess, along with a large team of civil servants. As well as sorting out the accounts, they put a stop to the great Irish families creating their own laws. From now on, the government in Ireland would be controlled from England.

Chancing your arm

In 1492, yet another row broke out between the Butlers and the Fitzgeralds. The Earl of Kildare and the Earl of Ormond had a raging dispute, this time in St Patrick's Cathedral in Dublin. When the Earl of Ormond stormed off and locked himself inside a room called the Chapter House, the Earl of Kildare decided it was time to let bygones be bygones. To show his good faith, he cut a hole in the door and bravely thrust his arm in. It was clasped by the other man's hand, the door was opened and the two men hugged, ending the dispute. If you fancy chancing your arm, the hole remains in the door today.

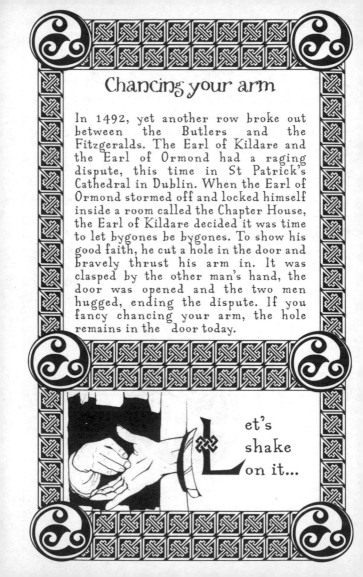

Let's shake on it...

CHAPTER THREE

THE ENGLISH TAKE CHARGE

Henry VIII

The English King Henry VIII is famous for divorcing, beheading and generally behaving badly towards his six wives. He didn't treat Ireland much better. It all started when Henry tried to divorce his first wife, Catherine of Aragon, who was too old to give him a son. Henry was a man who liked to get his own way, so when the Pope refused to allow the divorce, Henry ignored him. In retaliation, the Pope excommunicated him, which meant that Henry's soul could never go to heaven. In those times, this was just about the scariest thing that could happen to you.

In 1533, Henry solved the problem by creating the Church of England. His new church was Protestant, thus joining other churches in Europe that had broken away from the Pope. As the head of his very own church, Henry could make his divorce legal. He also had an excuse to plunder the Catholic monasteries and seize their land. In England, most people put up with this, as the Catholic Church had a reputation for grabbing money from the poor.

In Ireland, Henry tried to use the land he had grabbed from the monasteries to win over the Gaelic chieftains and Norman lords. Any lord who promised to be loyal to him could buy a large chunk of land at a bargain price. Most Irish people, however, supported the Pope and wanted to stay Catholic. The Catholic monasteries had played a very important part in their lives, especially in the countryside where the old Gaelic traditions were strong. Part of Henry's plan, however, was to make Ireland into another England, wiping out its language and customs. Henry tried to force the Irish to become Protestants by sending in his army. Even the Dublin parliament, usually

loyal to the crown, resigned in protest. So Henry thought up another plan – fining Catholics for not going to a Protestant church. The Irish simply paid up and stayed away. Henry's scheming had backfired: many of the Norman lords, who at first wanted to remain Catholic but loyal to the English crown, now joined the Irish rebels.

Death by poetry

Even in the late Middle Ages, poets were seen as holy figures in Ireland. Many people believed they had magical powers. The poet Niall O'Higgin was said to have killed Sir John Stanley (Lord Lieutenant of Ireland) with a curse in revenge for being robbed by Stanley's men. True or not, the English parliament in Dublin realised that poets were stirring up trouble, so in 1537 they created a law banning poets from travelling around Ireland.

Revolt!

Garrett Og Fitzgerald, the Earl of Kildare, had too much power for Henry's liking so he was flung into the Tower of London in 1532. Fitzgerald's son, 'Silken' Thomas,[1] believed his father was dead, so stormed into the Irish assembly and declared himself an enemy of Henry VIII. Thomas was joined by the usual line-up of Gaelic rebels, such as the O'Neill clan, but Thomas didn't have support from the Pope and the rebellion was soon put down.

When Thomas's supporters fled to Maynooth Castle, the Fitzgerald family home, King Henry's commander in Ireland, Sir William Skeffington, blasted the castle with cannons for seven days. He promised to pardon the rebels if they stopped fighting. When they gave themselves up, he went back on his word, hanging 30 of them and beheading another 25. As a grisly warning to other would-be rebels, he stuck their heads on spikes on the burned-out castle tower. Silken Thomas and his five uncles were hung, drawn and quartered a few

1 'Silken' got his name from the silk worn on his followers' helmets.

months later, in February 1537.[2] These events became known as the 'Pardon of Maynooth', a byword for English treachery.

Beg your pardon?

After Thomas's rebellion, Henry VIII ruled Ireland himself rather than relying on the Norman lords. From 1541 he called himself the 'King of Ireland', just in case any rebels didn't get the message. Most rebellious Irish lords were pardoned and given back their lands – but only if they gave up their Irish ways and became Protestant.

2 *An ancient prophecy had foretold the ruin of the House of Kildare if five sons of an Earl travelled to England in the belly of a cow – strangely, Silken Thomas's five uncles were taken to London in a ship called The Cow!*

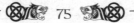

Are you dancing?

Whenever VIPs came to Ireland, they were met with dancers. Lord Deputy Sir Henry Sidney was won over by the sight of Irish women dancing jigs in Galway – 400 years before *Riverdance* swept the world with its twirls and high kicks. According to legend, some of the dance steps were made up by Druids leaping around in the woods.

Some dancers also claim that the unique style of Irish dancing, with the arms held firmly at the sides, was developed so that if English soldiers – on the lookout for banned Irish customs – looked into the window, they couldn't tell if anyone was dancing or not!

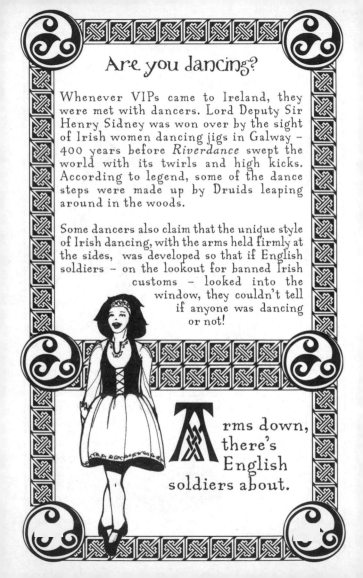

Arms down, there's English soldiers about.

Spuds and Spanish galleons

When Henry VIII's daughter Mary came to the throne, she wanted to return to Catholic ways. Unluckily for Ireland, she only ruled for six years and was followed by her younger sister, Elizabeth I, who was a firm Protestant. Elizabeth's Lord Deputy, Sir Henry Sidney, wanted to conquer Ireland once and for all, as the great forests of Ireland would provide timber for a fleet of new ships. He banned everything from monasteries to moustaches (a common disguise used by rebels). After defeating rebellious Gaelic lords in battle in 1575, he cut off their heads which he lined up along the path leading to his tent.

Henry Sidney

The Elizabethans turned the old Irish kingdoms into counties, each run by a sheriff. They then sold the land taken from the Gaelic lords to English soldiers and farmers. For years after, the English settlers were plagued by assassinations and massacres as Irish rebels took revenge. Meanwhile the English language was forced upon the Irish in laws, schools and place names – even Irish poets began writing in English. Soon Irish was spoken only among the peasants in the far north and west.

From Irish to English.

Irish wisdom

Though the Irish language was under threat, many Irish proverbs, known as *seanfhocail*, or 'old words', survived in English:

'Health is better than wealth.'

'An empty sack won't stand.' (Eat well!)

'If you lie down with dogs you'll rise with fleas.'

'An old broom knows the dirty corners best.'

'Men are like bagpipes: no sound comes from them until they're full.'

'A Tyrone woman will never buy a rabbit without a head for fear it's a cat.'

'A woman's tongue does not rust.'

'Every man is wise till he speaks.'

'Cattle in faraway lands have long horns.'
(The grass is always greener…)

'In the land of the blind, the one-eyed man is king.'

English officials dreamed up a new tactic: treat the Irish badly enough to make them revolt, then crush them. It worked. The Earl of Desmond, fed up with interfering English officials in Munster, asked the Pope for help. Soon thousands of Irish soldiers flocked to join the Earl of Desmond's rebellion, along with a force of 600 soldiers sent by Spain.

It gave the English just the excuse they were looking for. They wiped out the rebel forces, burning everything in their path. When the Earl of Desmond was murdered by the rival Moriarty clan in 1583, his head was sent to London. His huge estate was handed out to English officials.[3]

Meanwhile, England had become a great naval power, thanks to Irish timber and Queen Elizabeth turning a blind eye when her sea captains raided Spanish treasure ships. In revenge, King Philip of Spain sent a giant fleet of 130 ships, known as the Armada, to invade England in 1588.[4] It was met by the English fleet, whose small but well-armed ships ran

---

3 42,000 acres were sold to Sir Walter Raleigh, the English admiral.
4 The Pope offered Philip 1 million gold ducats to make England Catholic again (though he later backed out).

rings around the lumbering Spanish galleons. The Spanish Armada turned for home, only to be blown north, where it sailed into an almighty hurricane.

All washed up

Many galleons were swept towards Ireland. Though the English feared an invasion, the Spanish ships just wanted to shelter from the storm. In local legend, the shipwrecked sailors got on so well with the locals that to this day, people in south-west Ireland have unusually dark hair and olive skins. The truth is less romantic – over 5,000 Spaniards died on Ireland's beaches, killed by English soldiers or by Irish peasants for their fine clothes. There are Spanish genes in Ireland, but these originate from the first settlers (see page 15).

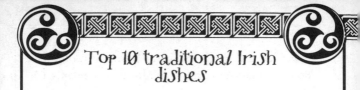

Top 10 traditional Irish dishes

A traditional Irish dinner isn't dinner without a potato on the plate. The potato was introduced into Ireland in the 16th century, possibly by Sir Walter Raleigh on his estate in County Cork. Another story suggests that the first potato was washed ashore from the Spanish Armada – the Irish often called the potato *an Spáinneach* ('the Spaniard'). Since then it has remained at the heart of Irish cooking, along with beef, pork and dairy products.

1. Boxty – A type of potato cake made from potatoes mixed with flour.

2. Barm Brack – Bread baked into long or round loaves and cooked with spices and fruit.

3. Colcannon – A dish made from cabbage or kale, potatoes, butter and milk. It was traditionally made at Halloween, and contained a ring, a coin, a thimble and a button. The ring meant that you would be married within a year, but a thimble or a button meant you were doomed to remain a spinster or a bachelor. The coin stood for wealth.

4. Crubeens – (Pictured right) Pigs' hind feet cooked with onions, seasonings and carrots. Crubeen and chips are still served as fast food in some country areas.

5. Drisheen – A black pudding made from the blood of sheep.

6. Irish stew – The one-pot wonder, made with potatoes, lamb, onions, herbs and stock. Traditional cooks insist that carrots were not used in the earliest versions of the stew, and shouldn't be used now!

7. Kale – A sort of wild cabbage that traditionally grew on sandy beaches in Donegal. Its large rubbery leaves are inedible, but the white stalks can be boiled.

8. Seaweed – Irish moss is a green or purple seaweed used to thicken soups and make jellies. Carrageen blancmange is made from Irish moss mixed with sugar, lemon juice and milk.

9. Tripe – Tripe, or sheep's stomach, was once commonly eaten on a Saturday night. It was usually sliced and cooked with onions in plenty of milk.

10. Oatmeal biscuits – Biscuits made over 1,300 years ago were discovered at a ringfort in Lisleagh, Co. Cork.

The flight of the Earls

King Philip of Spain didn't give up. Hoping to use Ireland as a base to attack England, he sent two more Armadas in 1596 and 1597. Both were wrecked by storms, so Philip sent another 4,000 soldiers to support a rebellion in the north. This was led by Hugh O'Neill, the Earl of Tyrone. Although O'Neill was a favourite at the court of Elizabeth I, he was secretly planning a rebellion. His agents smuggled gunpowder into Ireland in barrels marked 'Best English Beer' and he used lead intended for a new roof to make bullets. O'Neill was also a shrewd commander and his troops were well trained and well armed.[5] In 1598, he defeated an English army at the Battle of the Yellow Ford, then headed south, calling on other Gaelic lords to join the rebellion.

Realising the danger, Elizabeth sent her best general, Lord Mountjoy, who arrived in Ireland with a huge army in 1600. A year later, the Spanish fleet and troops arrived, not off the north coast but far to the south at Kinsale.

5 They were the first rebels to wear uniforms – red coats given to O'Neill by the English while his army was still loyal!

They were quickly surrounded by the English. After marching hundreds of miles south across mountains and bogs to join forces with the Spanish, O'Neill's soaked and weary troops were no match for the English cavalry. On Christmas Eve 1601 the rebel army was defeated and the Spanish sailed back to Spain.

Mountjoy's troops burned the fields in the south then stopped farmers from planting the next year's crops. The resulting famine was so severe that people were forced to eat nettles and rotting animals to stay alive. Any Catholic priests who had joined the rebels were used for target practice, dragged behind horses or simply trussed up and thrown into the sea.

Battle of the Yellow Ford

The harp

Lord Mountjoy's soldiers were also ordered to kill all harpists as Irish troops gathered round them before battle. The harp, the national symbol of Ireland, probably dates from around the 12th century. It faces left on letters from the taxman and right on a pint of Guinness. The first harps were square, before taking on the triangular shape we know today. An Irish harp is small enough to be held in the lap and the soundboard is carved from a single piece of bog wood. Medieval harpists were highly trained professionals who accompanied bards as they recited poems.

This guy was a real one-pluck wonder.

The original blarney

The word 'blarney', meaning smooth-talking or flattery, comes from the 16th-century Earl of Blarney, who was forced to swear an oath of loyalty to Elizabeth I. He gave such a long-winded speech that no-one could tell whether he was swearing an oath or rebelling.

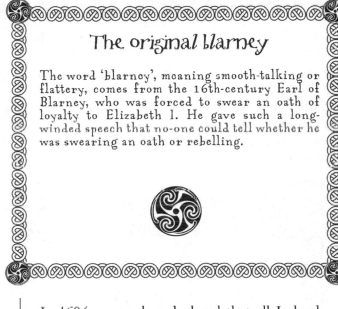

In 1604, a new law declared that all Ireland was now under English rule. This was too much for O'Neill and the other Gaelic lords of Ulster, and in 1607 they sailed to France – the so-called 'Flight of the Earls'. The days of the Gaelic chieftains had come to an end. James I, the new King of England since 1603, decided to sort out Ulster once and for all – again! He forced many Irish Catholics off the land and replaced them by settling, or 'planting', loyal Protestants from Scotland and England.

Rebels were banished to the bogs and hillsides, where many of them became outlaws and *rapparees* (bandits, named after the short pikes they used). By 1641, there were some 100,000 settlers in Ulster alone. The Protestants in Ulster had a different culture and history to the Catholic Irish: differences that were going to cause trouble in the future.

A few fleeing Earls

To hell or Connacht

In 1641, Ulster rebelled again, led by the O'Neill clan who wanted their lands back. It was a bloody affair. Thousands of Protestant settlers were slaughtered, including dozens drowned in Portadown, where rebels marched the settlers onto a wooden bridge before setting both ends on fire. In England, the public cried out for revenge, urged on by hysterical reports that wildy exaggerated the numbers killed.

However, England was caught up in a civil war between King Charles I (crowned 1625) and parliament, so the troubles in Ireland took a back seat. The Protestants in Ulster took matters into their own hands and fought back, killing hundreds of Catholics by throwing them over the cliffs at Islandmagee in 1642. Early in 1649, parliament won the English civil war and beheaded King Charles I. Its leader was Oliver Cromwell, a Puritan with strict Protestant beliefs. Nicknamed 'Ironsides', he wanted to stamp out any support for the royal family in Ireland. With the help of 20,000 troops, he quickly gained control over most of the country.

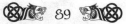

Ghost stories

After attacks on Protestants settlers in 1641, there were many tales of ghosts:

- Rebels guarding the River Bann would see ghostly heads floating on the water.
- An English woman dressed in rags and often holding a baby is said to rise from the water near Portadown wailing 'Revenge, revenge!'
- In Dungannon, a large woman stalks the town armed with a spear.

Revenge, revenge!

Fright night

Cromwell's soldiers showed no mercy, slaughtering the inhabitants of Drogheda and Wexford (most of whom were descendents of Norman and Elizabethan English settlers). Cromwell also did his best to destroy the Catholic church: looting churches, burning sacred books and forcing terrified priests to go into hiding. By April 1653, the war was over. The English parliament banned Catholics from owning land. Thousands of families were forced off their land all over Ireland. Cromwell gave them the choice of going 'to Hell or Connacht'.[6]

Battle of the Boyne

Even the English got tired of the strict Puritan way of life and in 1660 Charles II became king. He did little for Ireland's Catholics but there was a wave of hope when his Catholic brother James II came to the throne in 1685. James II was not a popular king and when a group of powerful English lords forced him to flee to France in 1688, the throne was handed to his daughter and her Protestant husband William of Orange, who became William III of England.

6 In Connacht, the rocky soil is bad for farming.

The bogeyman

The curse of Cromwell lived on – for centuries Irish mothers warned their children to 'eat up or Cromwell will get you.' Here are a few of Cromwell's infamous punishments:

- In Drogheda, the defenders of St Peter's Church were roasted alive while the commander of the town had his brains bashed out with his own wooden leg.

- Cromwell's men stuck the heads of Drogheda's leaders on pikes and sold the survivors to slave plantations in Barbados.

- At Bishops' Rock in Inishbofin, off the coast of Connemara, a priest was tied to a rock and his colleagues were forced to watch as he drowned in the rising tide.

- Priests in Wexford were flogged to death and their bodies flung into the sewers.

- In Wexford town, 300 women and children were slaughtered in the market place.

In Ireland, most people still supported James II. When he arrived in Kinsale with an army borrowed from the Catholic French King, he joined forces with an Irish army led by the Earl of Tyrconnell. In the city of Derry,[7] Protestants were terrified they would be massacred by the Catholic armies. Thirteen apprentice boys shut the gates of the city against the oncoming forces. When James II came to demand the surrender of the city, its defenders shouted the famous reply: 'No surrender.'

So began the longest siege in Irish history. For 105 days, cannonballs and mortar-bombs rained down on the city, while a barrier was stretched across the River Foyle, blocking supplies coming in from the sea. Some 4,000 people (about half the population) died of starvation or injury. Many survived on a diet of dogs, rats, mice, horses and seaweed. Finally at the end of July 1689, a relief ship sent by William III broke the barrier and provided food for Derry's inhabitants.

---

7 Also known as Londonderry, as the town and the surrounding county were given to emigrant Londoners in 1613.

William himself arrived in Ireland in 1690 with an army of 36,000 soldiers. When James tried to block William's route to Dublin, his army was defeated at the Battle of the Boyne on I July 1690, a famous date in Irish history. Despite this, Irish rebels fought on. At the Battle of Aughrim in 1691, 7,000 were killed by English troops and their leader had his head knocked off by a cannonball. The rebels weren't helped by the fact that their bullets were too big for the muskets supplied by the French.

The city of Limerick was the last place to hold out against William's forces, but it was forced to surrender in 1691. The resulting Treaty of Limerick left Protestants in charge, although it did promise freedom for Irish Catholics. But could they trust the English?

The marching season

In 1795, a clash between Protestants and Catholics at the 'Battle of the Diamond' led to the birth of the Orange Order, whose members swore a new oath to be loyal to the Protestant King of England. Every 12 July, the Orange Order celebrates William of Orange's victory at the Battle of the Boyne with a parade. However, by marching through Catholic neighbourhoods during the 1980s and 1990s, they often provoked violent riots. The bowler hats that are today often worn by members of the Orange Order were popular among English gentleman in the early part of the 20th century.

Chapter four

CATHOLICS vs. PROTESTANTS

The Penal laws

The Treaty of Limerick put a stop to violent religious wars in Ireland, but difficult times lay ahead for Irish Catholics. William III, the Protestant king of England, had promised to treat Catholics fairly, but before long Catholic lands were seized and handed over to his supporters.

Protestants only made up a quarter of Ireland's population, but they held all the power. Haunted by memories of the 1641 rebellion, they were convinced of a Catholic backlash. The threat of invasion by France

(a Catholic country) made things worse. In the early 1700s, the Protestant-run parliament brought in one tough law after another to keep Catholics in their place.[1] With the old Norman and Gaelic lords out of the way, there was no real opposition. These laws, known as penal or 'popery' laws, banned Catholics from:

- Carrying a sword.
- Owning a horse worth more than £5.
- Going to a Catholic school.
- Voting or taking part in government.
- Joining the army or becoming a lawyer.
- Playing Irish music or celebrating Irish festivals.

Protestants also took over many of the large Catholic churches. Catholic priests got around this by holding large open-air masses in the countryside, using lookouts to watch for approaching soldiers. They taught Catholic children in secret, in fields and barns, which earned these makeshift classes the nickname 'hedge schools'. Here story tellers and musicians taught Irish history and tradition, while dance masters taught pupils Irish dancing and fencing.

1 These laws also affected Ulster's Scots Presbyterians, or 'dissenters'.

Hedge school

Some educated Catholics made money from trading and banking in the small market towns that sprang up all over Ireland.[2] But in the countryside, especially in the south and west of Ireland, the poor were very poor. They lived in crowded stone cabins with thatched or turfed roofs and were the first to suffer when a series of famines struck in the first half of the 17th century. Famine soon led to disease. Though 'sweet Molly Malone', heroine of the famous song,[3] probably never actually existed, she may be the best-known of thousands of typhus victims in 18th-century Dublin.

2 A few wealthy Catholics became Protestants to keep their property.
3 'Molly Malone' was actually written by a Scotsman, James Yorkston, in the 1880s.

Irish superstitions

Despite all the battles over religion, many people still believed in ancient superstitions that existed long before Christianity arrived in Ireland:

- Rowan trees were thought to be lucky as they kept witches and evil fairies away. Sometimes a branch was kept in the house to prevent fires.

- People attached pieces of cloth to holy wells, following the old magic ritual of creating 'wish trees' by tying cloth to bushes.

- If one magpie appeared at your door it was a sign of death, while two magpies were a sign of good fortune.[4]

- A bunch of mint tied around your wrist was believed to ward off infection and disease.

- Women could become great beauties by rolling naked in the morning dew on May Day – the 1st of May.

4 *The first magpies arrived in Co. Wexford in the 1680s – blown across the Irish sea in a storm, according to Colonel Solomon Richards writing in 1682. The locals believed 'We shall never be rid of the English while the magpies remain.'*

Protestant landowners lived in big houses on beautiful country estates. Not all were born rich: William Connolly (1662–1729), who built a great mansion at Castletown, was the son of a blacksmith. Like many landlords, he had a second job in the Irish parliament. Other landowners worked in the army or owned estates in Britain. As a result, they spent little time in Ireland. These 'absentee' landlords were very unpopular with their tenants.

Connolly at Castletown

You should see my pad in London!

It didn't help that some young Protestant noblemen spent their time hunting, fighting duels and throwing each other out of windows. During the 1730s, Richard Parsons and other members of the Irish 'Hell Fire Club' in Dublin were famous for their wild parties and devil-worshipping. In one legend, a stranger who played cards at the club one stormy night had the cloven feet of the Devil himself!

The Skillelagh club

The Skillelagh clubs now sold to tourists as 'ancient Irish weapons' were never used in Ireland, though they were a weapon of choice among thugs in 19th-century London.

Protestants weren't all bad – during the 18th Century, there were no wars and the Irish population doubled. The road and canal network was one of the best in Europe and new farming methods made Irish livestock bigger and healthier. The growing linen trade brought jobs and money to Ulster, though there was little industry in the rest of Ireland.

In Dublin, the crowded medieval alleyways and tiny houses were replaced by the broad streets, elegant squares and grand houses[5] that give Dublin much of its character today. Protestant politicians wanted spectacular public buildings to rival those in London, so they also built a new parliament, the Custom House and the Four Courts building.

Four Courts

The black stuff

In 1756, Arthur Guinness opened the
Guinness brewery in Dublin, now
famous for its stout (a very dark beer).
Guinness was so popular that by the mid-
19th century, one in four Dubliners had
a job either in or connected to the
brewery. The Irish had been making
alcohol since around 1000 BC and the
first whiskey was probably made in
Ireland – the word whiskey means 'water
of life' in Irish. Ireland is also famous
for its poteen – a rough spirit (like
moonshine) made illegally from sugar,
treacle, or potatoes. It was sold in
'shebeens' – houses with a wedge of turf
hung over the door. Farmers were said to
give poteen to pregnant cows to help
them with their pregnancy.

'Patriots' and rebels

Like the Vikings and Normans before them, the Protestant settlers began to feel at home in Ireland. Towards the end of the 18th century, the Protestants eased up a little on their Catholic neighbours (but not too much). Some Protestants also decided it was time to rule Ireland themselves, without the British parliament meddling in their affairs, so they formed the Irish Patriot Party.

Meanwhile, on the other side of the Atlantic, American colonists had risen in armed revolt, defeating not one but two British armies during the American War of Independence (1775-83). Worried that the Irish Patriots might be tempted to follow their lead, the British agreed to give the Irish parliament more freedom in 1782. Its leader was Henry Grattan, a Protestant lawyer who had won support by passing a law allowing Catholics to buy land. Despite all their talk of freedom, however, Grattan and his parliament had no intention of giving Catholics any real power.

Secret Societies

Peasants, both Catholic and Protestant, were fed up at being pushed around by landlords and having to pay taxes (called 'tithes') to the Church. They formed secret societies with colourful names such as the Threshers, Rockites, Caravats and Ribbonmen. These societies provided a background to the creation of the United Irishmen by Wolfe Tone.

Members were bound by terrible oaths and were made to perform strange rituals (some involving masks and dressing up as women). They were led by imaginery leaders with names such as 'Captain Fearnought' and 'General Right'.

- In the south, the 'Whiteboys' attacked deer parks and damaged orchards, wearing white.

- In Antrim, visits from the Protestant 'Hearts of Steel' forced landlords to barricade their homes.

- In the north, the 'Oakboys' resented paying for roads used by their landlords.

- In Cork and Kerry, the 'Rightboys' included farmers and landlords, angry at having to pay church taxes.

- In Ulster, the Protestant 'Peep O'Day Boys' fought Catholic 'Defenders' in the bloody Battle of the Diamond in 1795.

Wolfe Tone, a young Protestant, had other ideas. Encouraged by the French Revolution (1789-99), he founded the United Irishmen in 1791. By uniting Catholics and Protestants who wanted to see Ireland as an independent state, he intended to drive the British from Ireland. Within a few years, the United Irishmen could boast 120,000 members from all walks of life.

The French, who were happy to make trouble for their old enemy, the British, offered Wolfe Tone their support. In 1796, an invasion force of 15,000 French troops appeared in Bantry Bay, County Cork. Storms prevented the troops from landing, but the sight of French warships off the coast of Ireland created panic in Britain and Ireland. Martello towers – forts built as a defence against a possible French invasion – can still be seen dotted around the coast of Britain. Soon British spies were busy rounding up the leaders of the United Irishmen. One man, William Orr, a northern Presbyterian who always wore a green necktie, became a rebel martyr after he was hanged in 1797. For many years afterwards, the rallying cry of the United Irishmen was 'Remember Orr!'

When Tone's rebellion finally broke out in 1798 the rebel army was scattered and confused. In Dublin, the revolt fizzled out in just a few days. The rebellion was strongest in Wexford, where rebels had a few minor victories, but its peasant army was wiped out by British forces at the Battle of Vinegar Hill. When the smoke cleared, some 30,000 people had died in the bloodiest event in Irish history. The French again sent a force to help the rebels. But they were too late to be of any use, and their ships were intercepted by the British navy, along with Wolfe Tone.

Wolfe Tone's rebellion

So near yet so far!

Ten bloody battles to remember...

1014   King Brian Ború ends Viking power in Ireland at the Battle of Clontarf.

1170   Dublin falls to Strongbow's Norman knights, beginning 750 years of English rule.

1260   The Normans defeat Brian O'Neill, the last High King of Ireland, at the Battle of Down.

1316   At Athenry, five Irish kings are slaughtered as the Normans stamp out Gaelic opposition in Connacht.

1318   Near Dundalk, Edward the Bruce's Scots-Irish army is defeated, ending a rebellion that threatened to push the English out of Ireland.

1535   Siege of Maynooth – with their castle blown to pieces, the the Fitzgeralds of Kildare, the most powerful family in Ireland, lose their wealth and status to Henry VIII.

1601	Battle of Kinsale – Hugh O'Neill's rebel army is defeated while the Spanish invasion force looks on. It's the end of the line for the old Gaelic lords.
1690	Battle of the Boyne – William of Orange defeats James II's army, dashing any hopes of a Catholic king of Ireland.
1691	Battle of Aughrim – James II's remaining supporters are routed.
1798	Battle of Vinegar Hill – Irish peasants armed with pikes stand little chance against 20,000 British troops.

...and one not so bloody battle!

1849: The Cabbage Patch Revolution. The Young Ireland rebellion in Co. Tipperary ends when the rebels trap a group of policemen in widow McCormack's cottage. They decide to fight another day rather than cause any damage to her home or her five children held inside.

There was a final flicker of rebellion in 1803 when 25-year-old Protestant Robert Emmet led an attack on Dublin Castle. It was a fiasco: only 100 rebels joined in and the attack turned into a riot. Emmet was caught and executed. Though his rebellion was a failure, Emmet inspired future generations of Irish patriots with a rousing speech at his trial: 'When my country takes her place among the nations of the Earth, then and not till then let my epitaph be written'.[5] To this day, the whereabouts of Emmet's body remain a mystery.

Battle of Vinegar Hill

---

5 An epitaph is the message on a gravestone.

A sticky end

- In 1681 Irish Saint Oliver Plunkett, was hung, drawn and quartered, the standard punishment for traitors. His preserved head is now kept at St Peter's Church in Drogheda.

- After his capture in 1798, Wolfe Tone cut his own throat to avoid the hangman's noose. Unfortunately, Tone made a hash of it and died a slow, painful death a week later. Sir George Hill, who was loyal to the English crown, commented: 'I would have sewed up his neck and finished the business.'

- In 1798, the rebel leader in Wexford, Father John Murphy, was flogged then hanged. His body was then burned in a tar barrel and his head cut off and stuck on a spike near the town chapel.

- In 1803, Robert Emmet was hanged in public. When his body was taken down from the rope, his head was cut off and brandished to the crowd.

Plunkett's head

The British parliament had had enough of rebellion. In 1800 it passed the Act of Union, creating the 'United Kingdom of Great Britain and Ireland'. From now on, Ireland would be ruled directly by the parliament in London.

There were some advantages to the Act of Union: being part of Britain's trading empire helped cities like Dublin and Belfast become wealthy. The number of people in Ireland rose from 2 million to 8 million between 1750 and 1841 and the country acquired a shiny new railway system. The first line, which ran from Dublin to the port of Kingstown (now known as Dun Laighoire), was built in 1834. By 1848, Ireland had 579 kilometres of railway. Nonetheless, in many areas, people remained desperately poor and though Catholics now outnumbered Protestants five to one, they had few rights.

Daniel O'Connell, a young nobleman and a brilliant speaker, helped poor Catholics to stand up to their landlords through a network of local priests. In 1828, he was elected a Member of Parliament, along with the other Irish politicians who now sat in the British

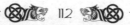

parliament in London. But being a Catholic, O'Connell was by law not allowed to take up his seat. The British government feared a rebellion from O'Connell's supporters, so a year later they changed the law and Catholics were finally allowed to enter parilament. Though this was a great achievement, poor Catholics (and some poor Protestants) were still not allowed to vote. So O'Connell set about breaking up the Union. He held over forty 'monster meetings' – huge, noisy gatherings in the open air – to show the British government that Irish people supported him.

Monster meetings

But many of his followers lost faith in O'Connell when, in October 1843, he cancelled a meeting at Clontarf to avoid a battle with British troops. O'Connell was arrested soon after and put in prison. Despite this, ordinary Irish people had learned that by joining together, they could bring about change. For the next few years, however, most of them were too busy trying to stay alive to do anything else.

The Great Hunger

When potatoes first arrived in Ireland, they were a wonder crop: not only did they provide food for 9 months of the year, they could be grown on almost any patch of land. They were nutritious too – in the 1840s, the Irish were on average 5 cm taller than the English! By the early 19th century, one in three people in Ireland ate almost nothing else. Relying on a single crop, however, was a taking a big risk.

In the autumn of 1845, when farmers went to dig up their crop, they were horrified to find their potatoes were black and slimy. The potatoes were infected with a fungus that spread like wildfire. Soon potato fields all over Ireland were a stinking, rotting mess. Worst affected were poor Catholics living in the west and south-west. Though people were very resourceful, eating nettles, seaweed, wild birds and even donkeys to stay alive, the poorest farmers were dying of starvation within a few months. When the crop failed in 1846 (and again in 1848 and 1849) the crisis became a catastrophe.

The British parliament knew what was happening but expected Irish landlords to deal with the problem. Though it funded work schemes for starving farmers – building roads that went nowhere and constructing piers where no boats could land – the wages couldn't keep up with soaring food prices. In the spring of 1847, soup kitchens were set up offering free bowls of 'stirabout', a watery soup made from meal, water and rice.[6] For most, it was too little, too late. By 1851, over 1.5 million Irish people had died and another 1 million had emigrated.

6 A few Protestant soup kitchens only served Catholics who promised to convert to become Protestants, who were then branded as 'soupers'.

In the 25 years after the famine, 3 million people left Ireland in search of a better life. Most went to the United States via Canada (the cheapest route). Irish emigrants were often treated badly, and in 1844, 40 people were killed during anti-Irish riots in Philadelphia. But there were jobs here for people willing to work with their hands – and anything was better than starving. By 1850, there were more Irish in New York than in Dublin and today, over 40 million Americans can claim Irish blood. Car maker Henry Ford was a direct descendant of a famine emigrant, while many US Presidents have Irish roots, including John F. Kennedy, Ronald Reagan and George W. Bush.

Some landlords took advantage of the disaster: teams of 'wreckers' evicted thousands of families from their homes for not paying rent. Forced to live in ditches, many wandered the roads until they dropped dead. Anyone caught stealing food was shipped to Australia, but hundreds turned to crime – at least in prison they were fed. The 'Great Hunger', as this time became known, changed Ireland forever.

famine horrors

- Anyone who ate the diseased potatoes got a terrible attack of stomach cramps and diarrhoea – enough to kill children and the elderly.

- Famine victims became human skeletons as they slowly starved to death. At Castlebar in County Mayo, people lay in the streets with green froth coming from their mouths as a result of eating grass.

- Famine led to disease. Typhus was known as the 'black fever', as its victims' faces became swollen and dark. Another deadly fever turned the victims' skin yellow. Scurvy, caused by lack of vitamin C, was called 'black leg' as it burst blood vessels in the arms and legs.

- Some Irish children also suffered from a disease that made their faces hairy while the hair fell out of their heads.

- Whole families froze to death in their cabins during the bitterly cold winter of 1847.

- Packed like sardines into boats known as 'coffin ships', thousands more died from disease on the month-long voyage to America.

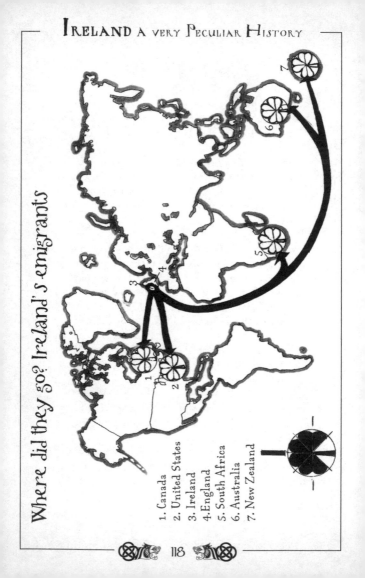

Where did they go? Ireland's emigrants

1. Canada
2. United States
3. Ireland
4. England
5. South Africa
6. Australia
7. New Zealand

Irish travellers

The 30,000 or so 'Travellers' in Ireland are a distinct people with their own customs, traditions and language, known as Cant. Though they call themselves 'Pavees', they are known as Travellers because they traditionally lived in caravans. No-one knows for sure where they came from: some say they are descendants of farmers forced off their lands by Oliver Cromwell or during the Famine. However, an old name for Travellers, 'Tinkers', first appears in 1175, so some families have certainly been around for much longer.

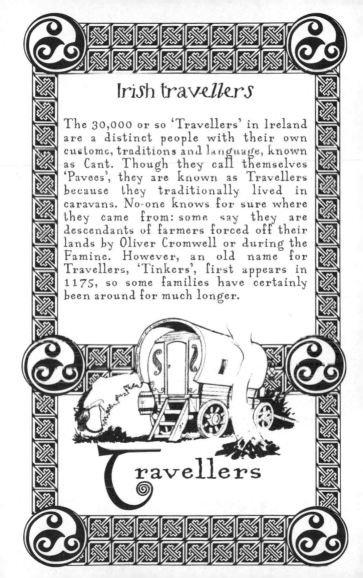

Travellers

Fenians, the 'land war' and Home Rule

There was enormous anger at both the British government and the landlords who had stood by while millions starved. During the Famine, Daniel O'Connell continued looking for peaceful ways to solve Irish problems. When he died in 1847, a new group, the Young Irelanders, decided that only violent methods would free Ireland from British rule. In 1842, the Young Ireland leader, Thomas Davis, started a very popular newspaper, *The Nation*, which linked the struggle for Irish freedom in the 1840s with the past battles against the Normans and English.

In 1848, the Young Irelanders tried to start a rebellion but it was poorly organised. While some of the leaders were captured by the British and sent to Australia, others fled to the United States. In the US, they told the world about the horrors of the Famine, and raised money for revolutionary groups that were to play a very important part in the fight for Irish independence.

Traditional music

Banned for centuries from speaking their own language, the Irish had long used music to help them recall their past. Every uprising inspired story songs, known as 'rebel music', which remembered the lives of fighters such as Robert Emmet or Roddy McCorley. Many rebel songs were written by Fenians (see following page), such as 'The Rising of the Moon', which describes the 1798 rebellion.

The oldest Irish tunes, known as *sean nós*, were sung by unaccompanied singers. Though some Irish folk melodies may date back to the middle ages, the vast majority of traditional tunes come from the 18th century, when jigs, reels and hornpipes were popular dance rhythms.

Turlough O'Carolan (1670–1738), the nearest thing to Ireland's national composer, spent over 30 years wandering around Ireland with his harp. Over 200 of his compositions survive.

On St Patrick's Day 1858, James Stephens founded the Irish Republican Brotherhood (IRB), also known as the Fenian Brotherhood, or the Fenians. Though opposed by the Catholic Church, the Fenians soon had thousands of members.

The Fenians worked in secret (some were spies in the British army) and carried out midnight raids on Protestant landlords under the name 'Captain Moonlight'. However, the British had their own network of spies, and when the Fenians tried to revolt in 1867, their leaders were quickly rounded up and executed. The year before, in June 1866, a bold group of Fenians (mostly ex-soldiers from the American Civil War) tried to invade Canada! They captured Fort Erie but retreated when British forces arrived. These Fenian raiders were the first to use the term Irish Republican Army or IRA, which was stamped on their uniform buttons.

One former Fenian, Michael Davitt, was more successful. He set up the Land League to help poor farmers who were most at risk during a famine. Members of the Land League

attacked or 'boycotted' (see page 126) landlords who treated their tenants badly or charged unfair rents, by refusing to work for the landlords or speak to them in public. This 'Land War' eventually persuaded the British Prime Minister William Gladstone to act: his Land Act, passed in 1870, ensured fair rents and made it easier for Irish farmers to buy and rent land.

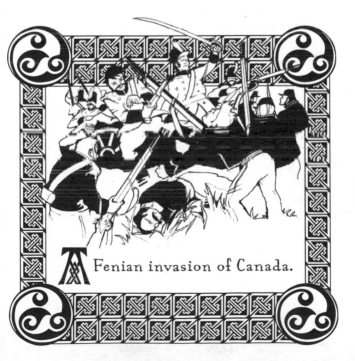

Fenian invasion of Canada.

The Land League's president Charles Stewart Parnell became a Minister of Parliament in 1875, with the hope that the League would encourage ordinary Irish men and women to get involved in politics. Parnell was a charismatic leader who wanted to take things further and achieve Home Rule: an Ireland run by the Irish, but with all the benefits of being part of the British Empire. To get everyone's attention, he and his fellow Irish MPs brought parliament to a halt by making long, boring speeches (one lasted 26 hours) and proposing time-wasting changes to new laws – a tactic known as filibustering.

At first, Gladstone was infuriated: in 1881 he had Parnell thrown in jail. When this made Parnell even more popular, Gladstone realised he needed to work with him to solve Ireland's problems. In 1886, the two men put together a Home Rule Bill to give Ireland a sort of independence. However, Protestants in Ulster, known as Unionists, wanted Ireland to remain part of Britain. Their MPs helped to stop Home Rule in its tracks.

Parnell was ready to try again when the news broke of his love affair with a married woman,

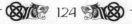

Kitty O'Shea. Though Kitty's husband had known about the affair for years, the scandal forced many of Parnell's allies to desert him. To add to his woes, Parnell was struck down by a fever. When he died in 1891, Home Rule had lost its great champion.

Irish words

When members of the Land League boycotted someone, they refused to work for them and completely ignored them in public. The word 'boycott' comes from Captain Charles Boycott, one of the first landlords to be boycotted, and is still used today. There are many other Irish expressions in English:

'pot-luck dinner'
(each guest brings a dish)

❊

' tying the knot'(see page 61)

❊

'taking the biscuit' – Taken from the Irish custom of 'cake dances'. Locals would gather at a crossroads for a party, which included a dance competition. The winning couple were given a cake or biscuit, which they shared with everyone else.

Irish words have also found their way into the English language, such as :

❊

playing truant (truaghan)

❊

being a hooligan (houlihan)

❊

being blown to smithereens (smidirín).

Quizzical

The word 'quiz' was invented by Dublin theatre manager James Daly in 1780, who bet that he could introduce a meaningless word into the English language in 24 hours. He hired gangs of schoolboys to write the word 'quiz' on the city walls. Soon all Dublin was dying to know what the mystery word meant!

That should set them guessing!

Question number one: What does 'quiz' mean?

Chapter Five

A NATION REBORN

The Gaelic revival

y the 1890s, life was less of a struggle for most people in Ireland. At the same time, many writers and thinkers felt that Irish ways were slowly dying out and being replaced by British customs. To help the nation feel more Irish, they urged people to rediscover Ireland's cultural past, its storytelling and music, Celtic art and the Irish language. At the same time, many outstanding Irish artists were inspired by Irish folklore, such as writers James Joyce[1] and Willam Butler Yeats and artists Jack Yeats and Sean Keating.

---

1 Joyce, like many Irish writers, spent most of his life abroad as he believed the Catholic Church had too strong a grip on Ireland.

In 1893, Douglas Hyde set up the Gaelic League. This encouraged Irish people to speak their own language. Many Irish speakers had died or emigrated during the Famine. By 1906, the Gaelic League had over 100,000 members. To showcase Irish plays, Yeats and Lady Augusta Gregory founded the Irish National Theatre, the Abbey, in 1903. In 1907, J. M. Synge's play, *The Playboy of the Western World*, caused a riot after the hero appeared to kill his father and get away with it.[2]

James Joyce

William Butler Yeats

2 *The play also shocked audiences by mentioning the word 'shift' – a type of women's underwear!*

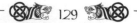

The Gaelic Athletic Association (GAA), set up in 1884, gave a boost to traditional Irish sports, especially hurling and Gaelic football. The GAA banned its players from playing or even watching 'foreign' (British) games such as football and rugby, which stopped many Protestants from joining. Rule 42, which banned non-GAA games being played at GAA grounds, was reversed in 2005.[3]

A hot drop

Some British customs became very popular. During the 19th century, tea was introduced into Ireland by wealthy Protestants. The nation was soon hooked and the Irish now drink more tea than anyone else – four cups a day on average. In Ireland, a proper cup of tea should be 'strong enough for a mouse to trot on'!

3 The Irish rugby team celebrated with a great win over the English at Croke Park 18 months later.

The First World War

When Gladstone's old party, the Liberals, came back into power in 1906, it seemed that Ireland would finally achieve independence. Not everyone in Ireland was happy about this. In the north, most Protestants wanted Ulster to remain British – at any cost. In 1912, Edward Carson had formed an army, the Ulster Volunteer Force, which had the slogan 'Ulster will fight and Ulster will be right.' Within a year, the UVF had smuggled in over 30,000 rifles for its 90,000 members. In the south, those who wanted Home Rule, known as nationalists, formed a rival army, the Irish Volunteer Force (IVF).

Some of the Irish Volunteers also belonged to more extreme groups. Sinn Fein,[4] formed in 1907 by Arthur Griffith, demanded a complete break from British rule (although at first it wanted to avoid using violence). The Irish Republican Brotherhood (IRB), which was made up of veteran Fenians such as Tom Clarke, believed in armed revolt.

4 Sinn Fein *(pronounced 'Shin fane') is Irish for 'ourselves alone'.*

Gaelic games

The British wanted Irish children to play 'gentlemanly' British games such as cricket. Yet Ireland has a unique sporting history of its own that stretches back thousands of years.

- **Hurling**: In the 13th century BC, the Tuatha dé Danaan defeated the Firbolgs in a 27-a-side game of hurling before wiping them out on the battlefield. In hurling, hurley sticks are used to carry and hit a small ball known as a *sliothar*.

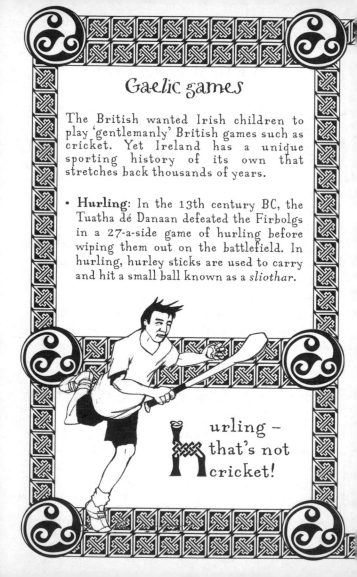

Hurling – that's not cricket!

- **Gaelic football**: The earliest accounts of this game date from 1670, though the modern rules are a mix of rugby and football.

- **Handball**: Along with hurling, handball was a popular team game played on saints' days in the 18th century.

- **The Tailteann athletic games**: A sort of Celtic Olympics, held at Tara from 632 BC until the Norman invasion. It was revived in the 1920s by the GAA.

- **Road bowling** (or 'long bullets'). It was played at Emain Macha, the ancient home of the Kings of Ulster. Players throw an iron bowl or 'bullet' along a country road. Whoever makes the distance in the fewest throws, wins the game.

Sinn Fein and the IRB both had few members but stockpiles of weapons, thanks to money sent by Irish Americans, who were still angry at the British government's failure to help Irish people during the Famine.

In Dublin, many workers joined the Citizen Army following violent clashes with the police during a strike in 1913. Its leaders were trade unionists such as 'Big' Jim Larkin and James Connolly, who wanted rights for workers as well as a free Ireland.

With all these different armed groups in Ireland, there was a real danger of civil war. Despite this, the British government planned to go ahead with Home Rule in September 1914. Then, with just one month to go, World War One broke out, with Britain, France and Russia on one side and Germany and Austria on the other. Over 140,000 Irish men joined the British Army, including many nationalists who believed that Home Rule would surely come when the war was over.[5]

5 By 1918, some 35,000 Irishmen had died in World War One.

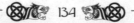

The Easter Rising

Many hoped that the troops would be home by Christmas, but the war dragged on. By 1916, some Irish Volunteers couldn't wait any longer for Home Rule. Most Volunteers were also members of the Irish Republican Brotherhood, and were supported by James Connolly, leader of the Citizen Army.[6]

Sir Roger Casement was put in charge of getting the Volunteers' weapons. Germany, which was happy to cause problems for Britain, offered the rebels 20,000 rifles. On Good Friday 1916, a submarine dropped Casement off on the Kerry coastline, where he waited for another German ship, the *Aud*, to deliver weapons and ammunition. When the *Aud* was intercepted by the British, its captain sank his own ship to avoid capture. Hearing this news, the leader of the Irish Volunteers, Eoin MacNeill, wanted to call off the rebellion. But a small group, led by Patrick Pearse, James Connolly and Tom Clarke, decided to go ahead with the plan, despite a lack of weapons.

6 *One of the IRB, John MacBride, just happened to be in Dublin for a wedding and joined the rising at the last minute.*

On the morning of Easter Monday, while most of the British army were enjoying the horseracing at Fairyhouse in County Meath, the group quietly took over the General Post Office and other key buildings in Dublin. The rising had begun. Pearse declared a Republic in the name of the Irish people. However, in the confusion, 4,000 Volunteers failed to take part. Those that did fight were mostly teachers and workers rather than soldiers. They fought bravely but had no chance against a force of 12,000 British troops armed with artillery and machine guns.[7] The Easter Rising had failed.

At first, the rising had little public support. The centre of Dublin was turned to rubble and many thought the revolt would put an end to Home Rule. The British reaction was swift – and ruthless. They executed 16 leaders of the rising, including James Connolly, who was so badly wounded that he couldn't stand upright for the firing squad. Some 3,000 Irish Volunteers and Sinn Fein members, many of whom had not taken part in the Rising, were jailed.

---

7 *The fighting lasted less than a week, though it stopped twice a day near the park of Stephens Greenit to allow the ducks to be fed.*

The Irish people were shocked and angry at Britain's actions. A wave of nationalism swept the country. British newspapers blamed the rising on Sinn Fein, who made the most of the publicity. In the 1918 General Election Sinn Fein swept to power, winning three quarters of the Irish seats in the British Parliament.

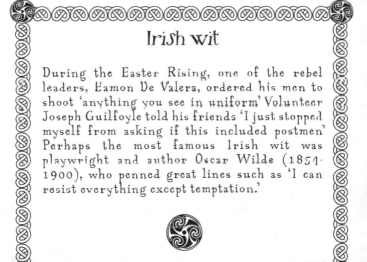

Irish wit

During the Easter Rising, one of the rebel leaders, Eamon De Valera, ordered his men to shoot 'anything you see in uniform' Volunteer Joseph Guilfoyle told his friends 'I just stopped myself from asking if this included postmen' Perhaps the most famous Irish wit was playwright and author Oscar Wilde (1854-1900), who penned great lines such as 'I can resist everything except temptation.'

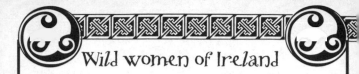

Wild women of Ireland

During the Easter Rising, rebel women smuggled weapons inside their clothes, knowing that British soldiers would not search them. They were part of a long tradition of bold and brave Irish women dating back to the Celtic Queen Medb (see pages 16 and 32).

- **Anne Bonny** (1700–1782) fell in love with a sea captain at the age of 16. Bored with life in port, she ran off with the notorious pirate Captain John Rackham, known as Calico Jack. Often dressing as a man, she was a great fighter and captured many ships with Rackham. Though she was caught by the British navy, she avoided execution and died in Virginia, USA at the ripe old age of 81.

- **Grace O'Malley** (1530–1600), the pirate queen of Connacht, used her private fleet of ships to control the seas along the west coast of Ireland. In one story, she kidnapped the grandson of an earl when he refused to invite her in for a meal. Her ransom was that he and his descendants would forever lay an extra place at the dinner table for her.

- **Countess Constance Markievicz** (1868–1927) was sentenced to death for taking part in the Easter Rising. When the British court let her off for being a woman, she said 'I do wish your lot had the decency to shoot me.' In 1918, whilst still in prison, she became the first woman to be elected to the British House of Commons.

- **Madeline 'Dilly' Dicker** (one of Michael Collins' many girlfriends). During the War of Independence, she sneaked onto a British mail ship to steal important letters going from London to Dublin Castle. She hid the letters inside her underwear then passed them on to the IRA.

Countess Markievicz in her Volunteer's uniform

The War of Independence

Instead of going to London, Sinn Fein's leaders set up their own assembly, or Dail, in Dublin. Michael Collins, known as 'the big fellow' and a veteran of the Easter Rising, also began organising a new rebel force – the Irish Republican Army (IRA). In January 1919, on the first day of the new assembly, IRA members in County Tipperary shot two policemen to provoke British forces. The War of Independence had begun.

The IRA worked in groups of 'flying columns' that carried out hit-and-run attacks on the police (the Royal Irish Constabulary). The police were the British government's eyes and ears, as well as being a good source of arms. To combat the IRA, the British brought in 8,000 armed policemen, known as 'Black and Tans'.[8] Many were ex-soldiers and they treated ordinary Irish citizens like an opposing army – shooting civilians and burning houses. Their violent tactics helped Collins to win support among the Irish people.

8 They got this name from their brown coats and black caps and trousers, which match the colours of the famously ferocious dogs from the Co. Tipperary hunt pack.

Bonfire night

In revenge for the British attacks on their homes, the IRA torched the homes of British supporters, especially the big houses belonging to wealthy Protestants. In one raid, the butler asked IRA members as they ran past with the furniture: 'Who should I say has called?'

On another occasion, when IRA members found an aged servant keeping watch on the property, they carried him outside before setting light to the building.

Perhaps the most notorious Black and Tan attack was carried out on 21 November 1920. That morning, the IRA had assassinated a dozen army and police officers in Dublin. In the afternoon, the Black and Tans drove their armoured cars into a Gaelic football match at Croke Park. When the spectators panicked, the Black and Tans opened fire, killing 14 onlookers and one player. To the Irish public, this looked like a savage act of revenge.

The British people were also shocked at the daily stories of police brutality. By the summer of 1921, over 1,400 had been killed on both sides, and neither side looked like winning. When Prime Minister David Lloyd George offered a ceasefire in July 1921, Sinn Fein and the IRA agreed.

Civil war

Arthur Griffith and Michael Collins went to London in October for negotiations with the British government. Lloyd George gave them a choice: sign a peace agreement, known as the Anglo-Irish Treaty, or face 'war within three days'. Knowing that the IRA had almost run out of ammunition, Collins signed in December 1921. The treaty divided Ireland in two: six counties in the north became Northern Ireland and remained part of Great Britain, while the other 26 counties in the south and west became the Irish Free State.[9]

When Collins returned to Dublin, he argued that he had done what was best for Ireland.

9 *In secret, Lloyd George told Collins he thought the other six counties would soon be forced to join the Free State.*

Though the Dail voted in favour of the treaty, many nationalists would not agree to an Ireland split in half. They were also furious that Irish politicians would have to swear an oath of loyalty to the British King. Civil war was in the air – between those for the treaty (led by Collins) and those against (the republicans, led by Eamon de Valera).

On 28 June 1922, the Free State army attacked the republican headquarters in Dublin and the civil war began. Free State soldiers were now fighting against their old IRA colleagues. And like all wars in which old comrades fall out, things got vicious – the Free State executed 77 republicans and put many thousands in prison.

Hundreds died, including Michael Collins, who was hit by a sniper's bullet during an ambush. The odds were stacked in favour of the Free State: their army had artillery and they knew the countryside as well as the IRA. Winston Churchill (who was at this time Secretary of State for British Colonies) even offered to lend the Free State aeroplanes to

help them fight against the republicans. In less than a year, the civil war was over, and Eamon de Valera announced it was time to accept the treaty and move on. After the civil war, many republicans found it hard to get work and emigrated to the US. For the next 80 years, some of these emmigrants would continue to support the IRA's campaign in Northern Ireland.

The bloody hand

Northern Ireland is made up of six of the nine counties of Ulster. The symbol of Ulster is the Red Hand, which comes from a famous legend. Two rival chieftains took part in a boat race to see who would become king of Ulster. The winner would be the first one whose hand touched the shore. When chieftain O'Neill saw that he was losing, he cut off his hand and hurled the bloody mitt onto the shore to win the race and claim the crown of Ulster.

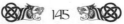

ONE ISLAND, TWO STATES

Northern Ireland

hen the civil war ended in 1923, Ireland at last had some sense of peace and independence. However, the two states created in 1921 – the Irish Free State and Northern Ireland – watched each other nervously across the border.

Protestants in the north were wary of armed Catholic nationalists. Their worst fears were confirmed when Michael Collins launched a secret IRA war against Northern Ireland in the summer of 1922, though this failed to protect the Catholic population. In the south, some people feared that Britain would use Northern Ireland to weaken the Irish Free State. They were right.

During the civil war, British newspapers primarily reported IRA attacks on Protestants (even though IRA members were mostly fighting each other). Protestants who were loyal to Britain – known as loyalists – took matters into their own hands. By 1922, over 500 people in Northern Ireland had been killed in clashes between Catholics and Protestants, and over 10,000 Belfast Catholics had been driven from their jobs.

Things got so bad that many Catholics moved south to the Irish Free State. Those who stayed in Northern Ireland were in for a rough ride. The voting system was rigged to make sure that Unionists held on to power. Catholics were kept under control by an armed police force, the Ulster Special Constabulary, which by 1921 had around 20,000 officers.

During the early 20th century, business had boomed in the north, thanks to the shipping and linen industries. In 1912, the Belfast shipbuilder Harland & Wolff finished building the world's biggest ship, the *Titanic*. But in the 1930s, competition from abroad meant that

jobs started to dry up. Tensions rose and in 1935 three weeks of rioting in Belfast left 13 people dead. Many Catholics were forced from their homes.

Thought to be 'unsinkable', the RMS *Titanic* hit an iceberg on 14 April 1912 while crossing the Atlantic.

It sank and 1,496 people drowned in the freezing waters.

Building a nation

Meanwhile, the Irish in the south started to build a country. The Free State designed its own bank-notes and postage stamps, and painted the old red British post boxes green. Many of the buildings and bridges damaged during the civil war were rebuilt and the Dail moved into Leinster House.[1]

The new government, led by William Cosgrave, wanted to calm things down after the civil war. It created a new unarmed police force, the *Garda Siochana*, and tried to make Protestants feel at home in the new state: they kept their jobs in the civil service and most Protestant landlords stayed on in their estates.[2] The new Irish flag symbolised the end of fighting between Catholics and Protestants. The flag's three colours were orange (for Protestants), green (for Catholics) and white (representing the peace between them).

1 *To show its independence from Dublin, the government in Northern Ireland built a grand new parliament building at Stormont in 1932.*
2 *Though IRA threats forced many Protestants living in border areas to move to Northern Ireland.*

Holy Control

The turmoil of the Great Hunger had made Ireland a very religious place. In the new state, older, 'magical' traditions such as bonfires, wakes[3] and holy wells began to die out. The Catholic Church played a big role in the Irish Free State:

- Divorce was banned, despite old Irish customs – see page 36.

- Books and plays with any violence or sex in them were banned – including many by famous Irish writers such as James Joyce, Sean O'Casey and Edna O'Brien. These strict laws remained in place until the 1960s.

- The first coins were going to show Irish saints. But the Church was afraid that if money was used for gambling it would upset the saints – so the new coins had pictures of animals instead (hare, salmon, cow and horse).

3 Wakes – a way of celebrating the dead – date back to Celtic times. Wakes were full of superstition: a window was opened to allow the spirit of the deceased to leave the room and sometimes people played cards, including a hand in for the dead person.

Building a new nation wasn't the only challenge – Ireland needed to catch up with the rest of Europe. There was almost 12,000 km of train track in Ireland during the 1920s, but the lines in rural areas such as County Donegal were narrower than the rest of the system so passengers had to change trains to complete their journey.

You wait ages for one, and then two get invented at the same time!

Ireland had no energy supply of its own, so the government built a giant power station on the river Shannon. Described as the 'eighth wonder of the world', by 1931 it supplied over 95 per cent of the country's electricity.

Many people hoped that having a good energy supply would create a boost for Irish industry, but Ireland remained a country of farmers. Farming was done the old-fashioned way – there were few tractors and cows were milked by hand. Farmers often received low prices for their produce, and so remained poor. With few new jobs in the towns and cities, people continued to go overseas in big numbers.

During this period of calm, the leader of the anti-treaty republicans, Eamon de Valera (known as 'Dev'), was waiting in the wings. He founded a new party, Fianna Fail, which promised to cut all remaining ties with Britain. When Fianna Fail swept to power in 1932, De Valera refused to pay back British loans that had been agreed in the 1921 Anglo-Irish treaty, claiming that the loans were payment for land stolen from Irish people in the first place by Britain.

A thoroughly modern Ireland

- The first transatlantic telegraph cables ran from Valentia Island off the coast of Kerry to Newfoundland. By the 1890s, Kerry was the hub of a global telegraph system, sending messages around the world in Morse code.

- In 1909, Ireland's first cinema, the *Volta*, was opened by the writer James Joyce. By 1930, Ireland had over 250 cinemas.

- By 1927, there were two radio stations in Ireland, known as 2RN (taken from the last line of an Irish song, 'come back to Erin'). These later became part of RTÉ, Ireland's national TV and radio broadcasting station.

- On 9 July 1939, the airline Pan Am's luxury Flying Boat, the *Yankee Clipper*, landed at Foynes on the Shannon river. It was the first passenger plane to fly directly from the USA to Europe. From 1939 to 1945, Foynes was the main airport for passenger flights between America and Europe.

In 1933, De Valera took a symbolic step further towrad independence – De Valera he changed the law so that Irish politicians no longer had to swear an oath of loyalty to the British king.

Ireland was soon in a 'trade war' with Britain. When Britain slapped high taxes on Irish farm goods entering the UK, De Valera got even by putting taxes on goods from Britain, especially coal and machinery. This looked brave, but it made life hard for ordinary Irish people, especially the farmers. This war ended in 1938: De Valera agreed to pay back some of the loans, while Britain gave up the right to use three Irish ports for its navy. A year earlier, the Irish people had also voted for a new Constitution[5] and the Irish Free State got a new name: Éire.

---

5 In the Constitution, the powers and duties of the government and the rights of its people are written down. The Irish Constitution has changed little since 1937.

The Blueshirts

The Blueshirts, later called the 'National Guard', were led by Eoin O'Duffy, the old head of police. Duffy organised marches, flags and salutes based on those in Nazi Germany. Fighting in the streets broke out between the Blueshirts and rival left-wing groups, but by 1937, the Blueshirts were disbanded.

Neutral but Poor

When World War Two broke out in 1939, Ireland remained neutral. De Valera wanted to show that Ireland didn't have to follow Britain's lead. He didn't want to side with Germany either, so when the IRA started plotting with the Nazis, the government executed nine of the IRA's ringleaders.[6] Would Germany have invaded Ireland? Documents (codenamed 'Operation Green')

found after the war showed that Hitler intended to use Ireland as a springboard to attack Britain. As it turned out, the invasion never happened – the German army was stalled by Russia.

Even if it had wanted to join the war effort, Ireland was in no shape to fight – there were just 14,000 badly equipped troops in the Irish Army. However, 70,000 Irish citizens and 50,000 from Northern Ireland fought for Britain during the war, and another 200,000 Irish people moved to Britain to work on farms and in factories.

In Ireland, the World War Two was known as 'The Emergency', and gave the government a good excuse to crack down on the IRA. The government started its own shipping firm to bring in supplies, but food was scarce and basic food such as butter, tea and bread was rationed. Because of low gas supplies, the state also created 'glimmermen' – inspectors who cut off the gas if someone used too much.

6 In the Christmas Raid of 1939, IRA members stole 1 million rounds of ammunition from the Irish army.

In Northern Ireland, farms and businesses supplied goods for the war, and its ports were used by British ships. In 1941, German planes bombed Belfast, killing over 1,000 people.[7] But Ireland escaped many horrors of a war in which 55 million people died and many cities were completely flattened.

At the end of the war, many of Ireland's old problems remained. Ireland declared itself a Republic in 1949, creating an even bigger split with Northern Ireland. This meant complete independence, with an Irish president rather than being under the authority of the British king.

The 1950s were tough times and many left Ireland to look for work in Britain: by 1961 there were just 2.8 million people in the Irish Republic, an all-time low. With help from America, living standards slowly got better throughout the 1960s. Ireland's appeal was helped by the visit of US President John F. Kennedy in 1963. The government's new *Taoiseach* (leader), Sean Lamass, did his best to boost Irish business by inviting in foreign

7 *Germany also bombed Dublin, killing 34 people.*

firms. The new jobs allowed more people to stay in Ireland and in 1966, for the first time in 100 years, the population grew. Lamass also tried to build bridges by meeting with Northern Ireland's new Prime Minister, Terence O'Neill. As the 1970s approached, many people were hopeful for Ireland's future.

John F. Kennedy

Irish generosity

In 2007, the Irish were voted the friendliest people on the planet. In the past, generosity to strangers was a basic duty and turning someone away was thought to bring bad luck.

- In the 17th century, pubs offered free food to anyone paying for a few pints of beer.
- In times of famine, private individuals went to great lengths to help out – the wonderful barn of Leixlip, Co. Dublin, was built in 1743 to provide jobs for starving farm workers.
- In 1946 and 1946, the Irish Red Cross brought over a thousand orphaned and homeless children from Germany, Austria and France to Ireland, where they lived with Irish families.

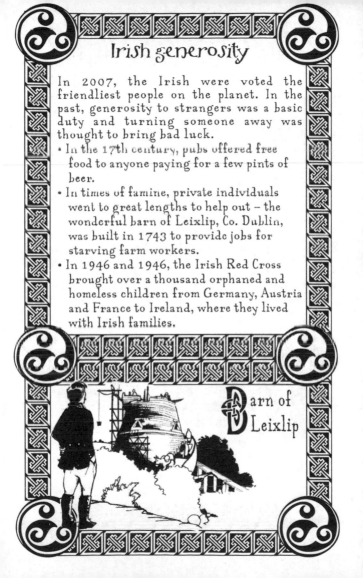

Barn of Leixlip

Ireland rocks the world

The Irish love affair with music never went away. While London throbbed to the sounds of the swinging sixties, Ireland's bands such as The Miami and The Capitol Showband were all the rage. Stars such as Van Morrison and Rory Gallagher started their musical careers in Irish bands, but went on to put Ireland on the rock music map. In the 1970s, many Irish groups sprang to success, such as Thin Lizzy and the Boomtown Rats, fronted by Bob Geldof. Irish rock got even bigger in the 80s with bands like U2, and on 13 July 1985, Geldof organised two Live Aid concerts that helped raise over $60 million worlwide for starving people in Ethiopia.

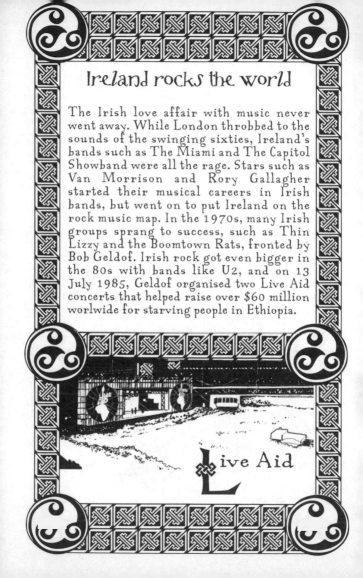

Live Aid

The Troubles

Things were not so good for Catholics in Northern Ireland, however. Protestants still carried most of the power in parliament, the police force and in business. It was hard for Catholics to get a good job. Many took to the streets, demanding the same rights as Protestants.[8] Unionist leaders, such as Ian Paisley, claimed that all the marchers really wanted was to make Northern Ireland part of the Republic.

In 1968, a Catholic march in Derry was attacked by a Protestant mob. Catholic streets in Belfast were attacked and set alight and the police did little to protect them. Many Catholics were forced to leave their homes. The British army was brought in, but the trouble did not stop.[9] The IRA began a bombing campaign, killing soldiers, policemen and civilians.

---

8 The marchers were inspired by Martin Luther King, the leader of the civil rights movement in the United States during the 1960s.
9 At first Catholics welcomed the army; this turned to hatred when it began raiding homes and throwing innocent people into jail in an effort to stop the IRA.

Some Protestant loyalists formed their own armed groups and killed many Catholics in revenge. Throughout the 1970s the fighting, known as the 'Troubles', got worse. On 20 January 1972, known as 'Bloody Sunday', 13 civilians were killed when British paratroopers opened fire on a largely peaceful march. Soon after, the British decided to rule Northern Ireland directly. But the violence only got worse: loyalists bombed Dublin and Monaghan in 1974, while the IRA took their bombing campaign to Britain.[10]

Dirty tricks were used by both sides and a low point was reached when ten republicans died on hunger strike in 1981. The British Prime Minister, Margaret Thatcher, had refused to meet the striking republicans' demands. In an act of revenge, the IRA attempted to assassinate Thatcher by bombing the Conservative Party Conference in Brighton in 1984.

10 The worst of the 'Troubles' lasted from 1969 to 1994. During this time over 3,600 people died and some 20,000 were injured.

Nelson loses his head

In 1966, on the 50th anniversary of the Easter Rising, the monument to English Admiral Lord Nelson on Dublin's O'Connell St was blown up by the IRA. The leftover pieces went on sale the next day. The head was stolen by students and rented out to pay off their debts. Today it is replaced by a towering 120 m spire.

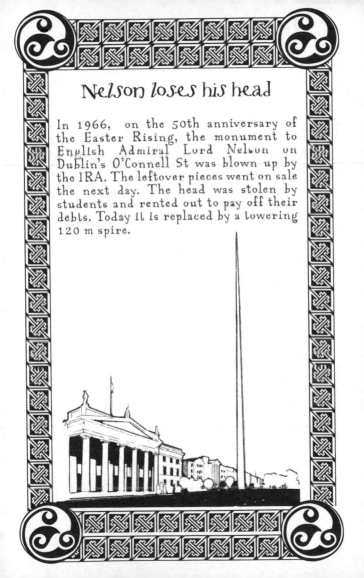

The Peace Process

A glimmer of hope came in 1985 when Margaret Thatcher and the Irish Taoiseach Garret Fitzgerald signed the Anglo-Irish agreement. The governments of Dublin and London agreed to work together to solve the problems of Northern Ireland.

Sadly, it was another 9 years before the IRA agreed to a ceasefire. An agreement was finally reached on Good Friday, 10 April 1998, thanks in part to help from US President Bill Clinton. It was signed by British Prime Minister Tony Blair and the Irish Taoiseach Bertie Ahern, along with Unionist leader David Trimble and Nationalist leaders John Hume and Gerry Adams, who agreed to share power in running Northern Ireland.

The peace was kept despite the bombing of Omagh by a rebel IRA group, which killed 29 people. It took a few more years for the IRA to give up its arms and for Unionists to accept the Good Friday Agreement, but by 2005 the IRA's armed campaign was over.

On 8 May 2007, a new government for Northern Ireland began at Stormont, led by unionist Ian Paisley and Nationalist Martin McGuinness. Millions watched the two former rivals sharing a joke on television. After all the years of bitterness and pain, few could believe what they were seeing.

The Celtic tiger

During the 1980s, the tough times returned – yet again young Irish people were forced to find jobs abroad. But by the end of the millenium, things were looking up in the Republic. Irish Taoiseach Charles Haughey told the country to tighten its belt (while at the same time lining his own pockets). People cheered in 1990 when the Irish soccer team, led by an Englishman, Jack Charlton, reached the finals of the World Cup.

In the 1990s, after centuries of economic strife, the Irish finally got a break. Business began booming, thanks to a little help from the European Union (around €50 billion) and big US firms who were tempted to set up shop

because of Ireland's low taxes. By the end of the 1990s, the 'Celtic Tiger' was roaring.

Life was good and the Irish suddenly had money to burn on big houses, big cars and expensive holidays abroad.[11] Many Irish emigrants returned to Ireland to work, joined by tens of thousands of workers from Eastern Europe and China.[12] Dublin was buzzing again and suddenly it was all the rage to be Irish. Irish culture – *Riverdance*, Irish pubs and U2 – took the world by storm.

At the beginning of our story, Ireland was a green and peaceful land, home to a few hunter-gatherers. For the next few thousand years, it was largely a nation of farmers who were in no hurry. Suddenly, Ireland seems to be hurtling towards the future.[13] Who knows where it will go?

11 The Irish were also getting bigger, eating more chips than the English and more chocolate than the Belgians.
12 Now more than 400,000 people living in Ireland were born abroad, and the population of the country has grown to 6 million.
13 In a recent survey of 31 countries, Irish city-dwellers had the fastest average walking speed!

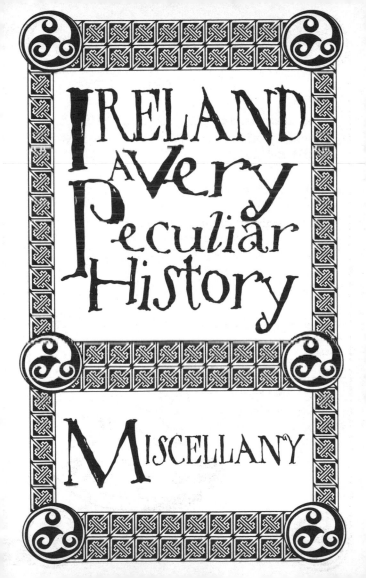

IRELAND
A Very
Peculiar
History

MISCELLANY

Recipe for cruleens (Pigs' feet)

This dish, traditionally served in pubs and taverns, takes some time to cook but is well worth the wait.

Preparation time: 15 mins

Cooking time: 4 hours

Serves: 4–6

Ingredients:

6–8 Pigs' trotters (preferably from front legs)
2 carrots
2 onions
1 stick of Celery
1 egg (beaten)
100g breadcrumbs
Salt
Pepper
Parsley

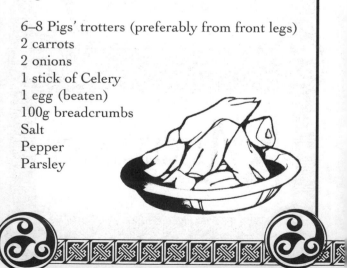

Method:

Rinse the pigs' trotters thoroughly. Place in a pot along with the carrots, onion and celery and cover with water. Season with salt, pepper and parsley, bring to the boil and simmer for four hours.

When the trotters are tender, remove them from the water and pat dry with some kitchen paper. Dip the trotters in the egg, and evenly cover them with breadcrumbs.

Under a medium heat, grill or roast the trotters for around 30 mins or until brown on the outside, but still tender on the inside.

Garnish with any spare parsley and serve with homemade chips or soda bread.

Timeline of Irish history

BC

6,500 Stone-age hunters arrive in Ireland from Spain, France and the Middle East.

4,500 The first farming settlements appear.

2,500 Beaker folk arrive – settlers equipped with some impressive metal know-how.

600 The celts come to Ireland and settle in.

AD

432 St Patrick begins his catholic mission.

c.550 Monasteries are established around the country.

795 The Vikings make their first visit and raid Colum Cille's monastery.

c. 850 The Vikings establish themseves in Dublin, Waterford and Limerick.

980 The Vikings are defeated by Irish lords at the Battle of Tara.

1005 King of Munster, Brian Ború, hails himself as the High King of Ireland.

1014 King Brian Ború ends Viking power in Ireland at the Battle of Clontarf.

1169 The Normans invade and take lands in the south east.

1171 Henry II arrives and claims Ireland for himself.

1258 Kings of Connacht, Thomond and Ulster challenge Henry II's rule and declare Brian O'Neill to be High King of Ireland.

1295 First Irish Parliament meets at Kilkenny.

1315 Edward the Bruce arrives and rallies Irish Kings against Anglo-Norman rule.

1316 At Athenry, five Irish kings are slaughtered as the Normans stamp out Gaelic opposition in Connacht: 11,000 slain.

1315–17 Famine hits, killing 1 in 4 people.

1318 Edward the Bruce's Scots-Irish army is defeated, ending a rebellion that threatened to push the English out of Ireland.

1322–25 Worst cattle plague on record.

1328 Crop harvest is destroyed, making the corn grow up 'white and blind'.

1348–50 'Black Death' kills many people.

1366 King Edward III of England imposes the Kilkenny Statutes – laws that forbid the adoption of Irish customs and language.

1487 With a little help, 10-year-old Lambert Simnel attempts to over-throw Henry VII, but his forces are defeated by Henry's army.

1534 Rebellion of 'Silken Thomas'.

1535 Siege of Maynooth – with their castle blown to pieces, the Fitzgeralds of Kildare, the most powerful family in Ireland, lose their wealth and status.

1541 Henry VIII proclaimed King of Ireland (as opposed to 'Lord').

1553 Accession of Mary I and the restoration of the Catholic Church.

1558 Accession of Elizabeth I and renouncement of the Catholic religion.

1588 The Spanish Armada attacks England. Many ships wrecked off Ireland.

1596 Earl of Tyrone, Hugh O'Neill, defeats the English at the Battle of the Yellow Ford with the help of 4,000 Spanish troops.

1600 Spanish troops capture Kinsale.

1601 Battle of Kinsale – Hugh O'Neill's rebel army is defeated while the Spanish invasion force looks on. It marks the end of the old Gaelic lords.

1604 New law declares Ireland to be under British Rule. Hundreds of British Protestants are 'planted' in Ireland to secure Ulster as English.

1607 The 'flight of the Earls' sees O'Neill and other Gaelic Lords sail for France.

1641 O'Neill's clan rebels against Ulster's 100,000 Protestant settlers. Hundreds of settlers are killed.

1642 Protestant settlers retaliate, killing hundreds of Irish Catholics.

1649 Oliver Cromwell wins English Civil War. Charles I is beheaded and Cromwell tries to stamp out Catholicism in Ireland.

1660 Accession of King Charles II.

1685 Charles II's Catholic brother, James II, becomes king. Catholic army formed under Richard Talbot, Earl of Tyrconnel.

1689 Seige of Derry lasts 105 days. 4,000 of Derry's protestant inhabitants perish.

1690 Battle of the Boyne – William of Orange defeats James II's army, dashing any hopes of a Catholic king of Ireland.

1691 Battle of Aughrim – James II's remaining supporters are routed. Treaty of Limerick pledges religious tolerance of Catholics under Protestant rule.

1695 Introduction of the first of many laws designed to oppress Irish Catholics – the Penal Laws.

1739 Severe famine hits, caused by failure of the potato crop. Thousands die, with the Catholic poor worst hit.

1756 Arthur Guinness opens the Guinness bewery in Dublin.

1775–83 American War of Independence.

1778 First relaxation of the Penal Laws.

1782 Henry Grattan appointed head of Irish Parliament.

1791 Wolfe Tone establishes the religiously tolerant United Irishmen, who call for an independent Ireland.

1795 Battle of the Diamonds leads to the establishment of the Orange Order.

1796 15,000 French troops appear on Irish shores in support of Tone's rebellion.

1798 Tone's rebellion flares but is quickly defeated by British forces. Battle of Vinegar Hill – Irish peasants armed with pikes stand little chance against 20,000 British troops.

1800 British parliament passes Act of Union, creating the 'United Kingdom of Great Britain and Ireland'. Ireland now ruled directly under British parliament in London.

1803 Robert Emmet leads failed attack on Dublin Castle.

1828 Lawyer Daniel O'Connell elected Ireland's first Catholic MP.

1829 Catholic Emancipation eases many of the restrictions forced on Catholics.

1842 Future Young Ireland leader Thomas Davis sets up popular pro-independence paper *The Nation*.

1845 Potato crop hit heavily by fungus, resulting in food shortages.

1846 Potato crop fails again. Corn Laws repealed.

1847 Daniel O'Connell dies.

1848 Devastating famine hits, killing 1.5 million people by 1851. Around 1 million Irish emigrate. The Young Irelanders attempt a rebellion.

1849 The Young Ireland rebellion ends when the rebels get trapped in a cottage in widow McCormick's cabbage patch.

1858 James Stephens starts the Irish Republican Brotherhood (IRB) – also known as the Fenians.

1867 Attempted rebellion by the Fenians is quickly stopped by British forces.

1870 Land Act passed, which ensures fair rent and makes it easier for Irish farmers to rent and buy land.

1875 The Land League's president Charles Parnell becomes an MP and campaigns for Home Rule.

1879 Michael Davitt forms the Land League to help starving tenants.

1886 Home Rule is drawn up by William Gladstone and Parnell to give Ireland a form of independence, but it is not passed because of resistance from Unionists.

1893 Second Home Rule Bill rejected. Douglas Hyde sets up the Gaelic League.

1910 William Gladstone's Liberal party voted back into power.

1907 Sinn Fein, formed by Arthur Griffith, demands complete independence from British rule.

1912 Third Home Rule Bill introduced. Belfast ship builders Harland and Wolff finish building the *Titanic*. Ulster Volunteer Force (UVF) formed.

1913 Workers clash with police during a strike. Many workers join the Citizens' Army.

1914 World War One begins, and Home Rule is postponed.

1916 The Easter Rising. James Connolly, Patrick Pearse and Tom Clarke seize a post office, sparking a rebellion. British forces shoot 16 leaders and jail 3,000 supporters.

1918 General Election. Sinn Fein wins three-quarters of the Irish seats in British Parliament.

1919 The Irish Republican Army (IRA) shoots dead two policemen, sparking Ireland's War of Independence.

1920 Government of Ireland Act, passed by the British government, establishes two parliaments: one for the six counties of Northern Ireland, and another for the remaining 26 counties.

1921 Anglo-Irish Treaty signed. The six counties of Northern Ireland remain part of Britain, while the other counties become the Irish Free State.

1922 After some nationalist opposition to the terms of the Anglo-Irish treaty, the Free State Army attacks the republican headquarters in Dublin. Civil war begins.

1922 The IRA launches an unsuccessful secret war against Northern Ireland.

1923 Civil war ends.

1932 Eamon de Valera's party Fianna Fail wins power in the Irish Free State parliament and promises to cut all remaining ties with Britain.

1935 Three weeks of rioting in Belfast leave 13 people dead.

1937 The Irish people vote for a new constitution. Irish Free State renamed Éire.

1938 Britain and Éire sign agreement that ends the trade wars.

1939 World War Two begins. Northern Ireland joins Britian's war effort, whilst Éire chooses to remain neutral.

1941 German planes bomb Belfast, killing over 1,000 people.

1949 Éire declares itself the Republic of Ireland.

1959 De Valera becomes president of the Republic of Ireland.

1961 Population of the Irish Republic hits an all-time low – 2.8 million people.

1966 Thanks to US support, the population of the Irish Republic grows for the first time in 100 years.

1968 A Catholic march in Derry is attacked by a Protestant mob, sparking violent unrest between Catholics and loyalist Protestants.

1972 Bloody Sunday. On 20th January, 13 civilians are killed by British paratroopers during a largely peaceful march.

1974 Loyalists bomb Dublin and Monaghan while the IRA bombs parts of Britain.

1981 Ten republicans die on hunger strike when the British Prime Minister, Margaret Thatcher, refuses to meet their demands.

1984 The IRA bombs the Conservative party conference in Brighton in an attempt to assassinate Margaret Thatcher.

1985 British PM Margaret Thatcher and Irish Taoseach Garret Fitzgerald sign the Anglo-Irish Agreement in a bid for the two opposing sides to settle Northern Ireland's problems together.

1990 Republic of Ireland's football team reaches the World Cup final.

1994 The IRA agrees to a cease-fire.

1997 Despite opposition from the Roman Catholic church, divorce becomes legal in Ireland under some circumstances.

1998 Good Friday Agreement signed on 10 April by British PM Tony Blair and Irish Taoseach Bertie Ahern as well as Unionist leader David Trimble and nationalist leaders

John Hume and Gerry Adams. Omagh bombing, 15 August.

2002 Irish Republic's currency, the Punt, is replaced by the Euro.

2005 IRA's armed campaign is considered to be over.

2007 (8 May) A new government for Northern Ireland is established, led by unionist leader Ian Paisley and nationalist leader Martin McGuinness.

2007 (June) Coalition formed between Fianna Fáil, the Progressive Democrats, the Green party and some independents.

2008 Prime Minister Bertie Ahern announces he is to resign.

2009 Plans to compensate the victims of violence during the Troubles spark controversy.

Celtic names

A
Aengus [Ang-gus]
Aillen [Allen]
Ankou [Ann-koo]

B
Beli [Bell-ee]
Beltane [Bell-tayn]
Bres [Bresh or Bress]

C
Cailleach Bheur [Call-ee Vaar]
Calatin [Call-ah-tin]
Cathbad [Kah-bud or Cuth-bert]
Conchobar [Connor]
Cúchulainn [Coo-hull-in or Coo-shull-in]
Culann [Coo-lann]
Cumhaill [Cool]

D
Danu [Dan-noo or Day-noo]
Dechtire [Deck-tir-ra]
Diarmaid [Der-mot

E
Eochaid [Yoch-hee]
Etain [Ee-taw-in]

F
Fedlimid [Fail-im-ee]
Fiacha [Fee-ach-ah]
Fianna [Fee-ann-a]
Finngeas [Fin-gus]
Fintan [Fin-tan]
Fir Bholg [Fear Volg]
Fuamnach [Foo-um-nach]

G
Gaels [Gaylz]
Glashtin [Glash-tinn]
Grainne [Graw-nyah]

L
Lugh [Lou]

M
Macha [Mock-ah]
MacCumhaill [MacCool]
Maug Mollach [Meg Moll-ack]
Medb [Maeve]
Morrigan [Morr-ee-gan]
Muirne [Morna]

N
Naoise [Nee-shee]
Nechtan [Neck-tann]
Nemed [Nemm-eth]
Nynnyaw [Nynn-yow]
Nuada [Noo-ah-da]

Q
Quayle [Kwayl]

S
Samhain [Sam-ayn]
Sava [Sah-vah]
Scathach [Scah-hah]
Sceolan [Skyo-lin]
Setanta [Set-ann-tah]

T
Tir Nan Og [Tear-nan-Ogg]
Tuatha Dé Danaan [Tootha Day Dann-ann]
Tuiren [Toor-enn]

Index

A

absentee landlords 100
Act of Union 112, 173
Adams, Gerry 164, 179
Ahern, Bertie 164, 179, 180
America *see also* USA 43, 104, 117, 153, 158
American War of Independence 104
Annals of Connacht 64
Anglo-Irish Agreement 164, 179
Anglo-Irish Treaty 142, 145, 177
Antrim 10, 33, 43, 105
Ardagh Chalice 37
Aud 135
Australia 116, 118, 120

B

banshees 47
Barn of Leixlip 159
battles
  Aughrim 94, 109, 172
  Bannockburn 61
  Boyne 8, 9, 91, 94, 95, 109, 172
  Clontarf 8, 49, 108, 149
  Diamond 95, 105, 186

Tara 49, 168
Vinegar Hill 8, 107, 109, 110, 173
Yellow Ford 8, 9, 85, 171
Beaker folk 19
Belfast 8, 112, 147, 148, 157, 161, 177, 178
Black and Tans 140, 141
Black Death 62, 63, 170
Blair, Tony 164, 179
Blarney 88
Bloody Sunday 162, 178
Blueshirts 155
Bonny, Anne 138
Book of Invasions 28
Book of Kells 37
Brehon law 23, 32
Brendan, St 41
Brian Ború 49,108, 169
Brigid 35
Brigid, St 41, 42, 54
Britain 12, 13, 15, 33, 38, 26, 33, 46, 100, 106, 112, 124, 134, 135, 142, 146, 154, 156, 157, 162, 177
British Army 121, 134, 132, 161
Bronze Age 19–20
Butler family 68, 70

C

Cabbage-patch
  Revolution
  8, 9, 109, 174
Canada 116, 121, 118
'Captain Moonlight' 121
Carson, Edward 131
Casement, Roger 135
Castletown mansion 100
Catholicism 72, 73, 77,
  85, 87–89, 91–95,
  96–128, 146– 162, 170,
  171, 174, 179
Céide field 15
Celtic
  art 24, 128
  gods 26, 34, 35
  names 181–183
Celts 21–25, 28–30, 32,
  57, 168
'chancing your arm' 69
changelings 47
Charles I 89, 171
Charles II 91, 172
chieftains 20, 30, 33, 44,
  48, 49, 51, 54, 55, 61, 62,
  69, 72, 87, 144
Christianity 33, 36, 38,
  49, 99
Churchill, Winston 143
Citizen Army 134, 135
Civil war 134, 142–144,
  146, 147, 149, 177
Clarke, Tom 135, 176
Clinton, Bill 164

'coffin ships' 117
Collins, Michael 139, 140,
  142–143, 146
Colum Cille 38, 43, 168
Connacht 9, 16, 22, 32,
  36, 57, 59, 61, 62, 169
Connolly, James
  134–136, 176
Connolly, William 100
Conservative Party
  Conference 162, 179
Cork 8, 17, 19, 28, 46,
  82, 83, 106, 107
Cosgrave, William 149
crannogs 32
Croke Park 140, 141
Cromwell, Oliver 89–92,
  171
Cúchulainn 25, 26, 32, 35
curses 50

D

Dagda 34, 35
Dail 140, 142, 149
Davis, Thomas 120, 174
Davitt, Michael 123, 125
Derry 13, 93, 161, 178
De Valera, Eamon 137,
  143, 154, 155, 156, 177,
  178
Dian Cecht 35
Dicker, Madeline 139
Drogheda 8, 55, 91, 92,
  111
druids 33–34, 35, 76

Dublin 6, 8, 46, 48, 49, 53, 55, 57–59, 64, 66, 69, 70, 72, 73, 94, 98, 101–103, 107, 108, 110, 112, 116, 127, 134–136, 139–148, 149, 157, 162, 163, 166, 168, 169, 172, 173

Dublin castle 110, 139, 173

Dún Aonghasa 19

E

Easter Rising 135–137, 138, 139, 140, 162, 176

Edward III 66, 170

Edward VI 68

Edward the Bruce 62, 108, 169

Éire 24, 154, 177, 178

Elizabeth I 77, 80, 84, 89, 91, 170

English Civil War 89, 171

Emain Macha 32, 36, 133

'Emergency' 157

emigration 112, 115, 116, 118, 129, 144, 166, 174

Emmet, Robert 110, 111, 121, 173

Europe 11, 12, 15, 24, 29, 38, 48, 72, 102, 151, 153, 165, 166

F

famine 19, 62, 64, 65, 85, 95, 98, 112, 114–119, 120, 123, 129, 134, 159, 169, 172, 174

Fenians 121–123, 131–135, 174, 175

Finn MacCool 10, 26, 27

Fitzgerald, Garret 164, 179

Fitzgeralds (of Kildare) 68, 70, 74, 108, 170

'Flight of the Earls' 84, 87, 88

Four Courts 102

France 8, 13, 15, 38, 51, 58, 87, 91, 94, 97, 106, 134, 159, 168, 171, 173

G

Mount Gabriel 19

Gaels *see* Celts

Gaelic Athletic Association (GAA) 130

Gaelic football 130, 133, 141

Gaelic League 129, 175

gallowglasses 61

General Election (1918) 135, 176

Germany 48, 132, 135, 155, 156, 157, 159

ghost stories 90

Gladstone, William

123–124, 131, 175
Glendalough monastery 45
'glimmermen' 157
Good Friday Agreement 164, 179
Grattan, Henry 104
Great Hunger 114–119
green martyrs 42
Griffith, Arthur 131, 142, 175
Guinness 87, 102, 172

H

Haughey, Charles 165
hedge school 97, 98
Hell Fire Club 101
Henry II 51, 53, 54, 169
Henry VII 68, 69
Henry VIII 71–75, 108, 170
hillforts 19, 32
Hume, John 164, 179
hunger strike 162, 179
Hurling 66, 130, 132
Hyde, Douglas 129, 175

I

Ice Age 11–12
Inish Mór 19
Irish dancing 75, 97
Irish Free State 142–143, 146, 147, 149, 150, 154, 177
Irish National Theatre 129
Irish Republican Army (IRA) 122, 139, 140–144, 146, 147, 156, 157, 161–164, 176, 177, 178, 179, 180
Irish Republican Brotherhood (IRB) see Fenians
Irish Sea 12, 99
Irish Volunteer Force (IVF – also Irish Volunteers) 131, 135, 136, 137, 139

J

James I 87
James II 91, 93, 94, 109
Joyce, James 128, 129, 150, 153

K

Kennedy, John F. 158
Kieran, St 41
Kilkenny 55, 56
Kilkenny Statutes 66, 67, 170

L

Lamass, Sean 158
Land Act 123, 175
Land League 123–124, 126
Land War 123

Leinster 9, 22, 54
Liberals 131
Liffey river 46, 49
Lloyd George, David 142
London 61, 65, 74, 75, 80, 101, 102, 112, 113, 139, 140, 142, 160, 164, 173
loyalists 147, 162, 178

M

MacMurrough, Dermot 51–52, 54
Markievicz 139
marriage 62
Mary I 77, 170
Maynooth Castle 74
Mayo 15, 59, 117
McGuinness, Martin 165, 180
Meath 9, 17, 22, 31, 54, 59, 136
Medb 16, 32, 138
megalithic tombs 17, 18, 29
Monaghan 162, 178
monasteries 37, 38, 40, 41, 43, 44, 45, 72, 77, 168
monster meetings 113
Moriarty clan 80, 189
Munster 9, 22, 29, 49, 80

N

Nation, The 129, 174
nationalists 131, 132, 143, 146, 165, 177, 179, 180
Nazis 155, 156
Newgrange 17, 18
Niall of the Nine Hostages 26
Normans 51, 55, 56, 58, 59, 60–62, 66, 68, 72, 75, 91, 97, 108, 169
Northern Ireland 42, 44, 146–1148, 149, 156, 157, 158, 161, 162, 164, 176, 177, 178, 179, 180
Nuada 23, 183

O

O'Connell, Daniel 112–114, 120, 174
Ogham stones 8, 29
O'Neill, Brian 61, 108, 169
O'Neill clan 62, 74, 89
O'Neill, Hugh 84–85, 87, 109, 171
O'Neill, Terence 158
O'Neill, Turlough 61
Omagh bombing 164
O'Malley, Grace 8, 138
Orange Order 95, 173
Orr, William 106
O'Toole clan 59

P

Paisley, Ian 161, 165, 180
Pale 66, 68
'Pardon of Maynooth' 75
Parnell, Charles Stewart
124–125, 175
Patrick, St 33–34, 36
Pearse, Patrick 135, 136,
176
Philip I (of Spain) 80, 84
'planting' 87
*Playboy of the Western
World* 129
Plunkett, Oliver 111
pooka 47
'Popery' laws 97
Portadown 89, 90
potato 47, 82, 83, 103,
114, 115, 172, 174
poteen 103
Protestantism 72, 73, 75,
77, 87–91, 96–127, 130,
131, 141, 146, 147, 149,
161, 162, 171, 172, 178
proverbs 79

Q

'quiz' 129

R

railway 112, 151
'rapparees' 88
ringforts 24, 32, 83
Riverdance 75, 166

Robert the Bruce 62
Romans 21, 29, 33
Ruadhan St 50

S

Mount Sandel 13
Saxons 60
Scotland 10, 13, 87
seiges
  Derry 93, 172
  Maynooth 108, 170
selkies 47
shanachies 28
Sidney, Henry 76–77
'Silken' Thomas 74–75,
170
Simnel, Lambert 68
Sinn Fein 131, 132, 136,
137, 140, 142, 176
skillelagh club 107
Skellig Michael 40
sligthi 22
Spanish Armada 80–81,
82, 84, 170
Spire of Dublin 162
Stephens, James 121,
174
'stirabout' 115
Stone Age 13–15, 17, 168
Stone of Destiny 30
Stormont 149, 164
Strongbow 52–53, 58,
108, 169
superstition 99, 149

T

Táin Saga 15, 24
Tara 24, 30, 36, 49, 50, 137, 168
Tigernmas 27
Titanic 8, 147, 148, 176
Thatcher, Margaret 162, 164, 179
Tone, Wolfe 106–107, 111, 173
travellers 119
Treaty of Limerick 172
Trim castle 55, 59
Trimble, David 164, 179
'Troubles' 161–162
Tuatha Dé Danaan 23, 28, 47, 132, 185
Tuathal 26

U

Ulster 9, 22, 32, 36, 61, 62, 87–89, 102, 124, 131, 144, 171
Ulster Special Constabulary 147
Ulster Volunteer Force (UVF) 131, 176
unionists 124, 134, 147, 164, 175
United Irishmen 106, 173
USA 120, 144, 138, 153, 158, 164, 165, 178

V

Vikings 8, 34, 43–49, 53, 58, 104, 108, 168, 169

W

War of Independence 139, 140–142
Waterford 46, 53, 63, 168
Wexford 8, 46, 91, 92, 9   9   , 107, 110
white martyrs 42
Wicklow 20, 45, 46
Wilde, Oscar 137
William of Orange 91, 93–96, 96, 109, 172, 75
whiskey 7, 103
World War One 131–135
World War Two 156–157
'wreckers' 116

Y

Yankee Clipper 8, 153
Yeats, Jack 128, 129
Yeats, William 129
Young Irelanders 120, 174

The Cherish Brothers
at university

The Cherish Family

'The Cherished Library' is a
definitive collection of
masterworks, beautifully
written, designed and
illustrated by the most
influential authors, artists,
designers and bookbinders of
their day.

These facsimile editions from
the world-class collection of
the Cherish family library have
been lovingly crafted to
recreate the authentic
look and feel of the
originals in the family's
much-loved library.*